Journey Man's Diary- Volume I

Journey Man's Diary- Volume I

Organizing, Developing, Changing

"We know the parable of the frog,
what we don't know is that we are the frogs."

Naushad H. Javaid

AuthorHouse™
1663 Liberty Drive
Bloomington, IN 47403
www.authorhouse.com
Phone: 1-800-839-8640

© 2011 by Naushad H. Javaid. All rights reserved.

No part of this book may be reproduced, stored in a retrieval system, or transmitted by any means without the written permission of the author.

First published by AuthorHouse   07/06/2011

ISBN: 978-1-4567-8248-1 (sc)

Printed in the United States of America

Any people depicted in stock imagery provided by Thinkstock are models, and such images are being used for illustrative purposes only.
Certain stock imagery © Thinkstock.

This book is printed on acid-free paper.

Because of the dynamic nature of the Internet, any web addresses or links contained in this book may have changed since publication and may no longer be valid. The views expressed in this work are solely those of the author and do not necessarily reflect the views of the publisher, and the publisher hereby disclaims any responsibility for them.

17/11/01

'I think most of my anxiety about them finding out that I'm looking for another job is imaginary. They are stuck in their own myopic world. So be it! However, I must be careful not to rock the boat, before my ship lands . . .'

PROLOGUE

How do organizations become more effective? I believe the answer is by making the people who make up the organization more effective, especially effective in working together and achieving the desired results together. How can we make the people more effective? My answer, by making them realize their potential and linking it with the organizational vision and ensuing objectives. This can be done by providing an environment, which enables people to shine and rise to the given challenge. Finally, the question, how can we create such an environment?

This is the point of exploration that I invite all the readers to delve in. When we talk about environment we are talking about the culture. In essence, what we are saying is that in order to perform at the peak; we need a culture, which makes it possible. Regardless of what organization development strategy is employed to do so, the change must start with the mindset of the people. This may be a tedious process, but in my view, it is the best place to start, and eventually the best place to end, if at all there is an 'end' in any cycle of improvement.

What follows is built around my observations in the corporate world. It may be subjective but, to me, it is very real. What is required is to live through it and come out with some answers and some clues as to where to begin and how to go about it. You may find some answers in there. However, it is more likely that you will come up with more questions. That will be good.

ORGANIZING, DEVELOPING & CHANGING

"Life just happens. You've got to learn to deal with It"-A friend

The Pocket Oxford Dictionary defines the word organization in the following way: Organizing or being organized; Organized body system or society. The same dictionary defines the word organize as such: Give an orderly structure to, systematize; make arrangements for; make organic; make into living tissue! In other words, the term 'organize' implies consistent change.

Organizing, then, is the act of continuously rearranging, and we organize to achieve something. In a business sense, our organizations are arranged to make money, and we keep on rearranging them as times demand. Change is inherent in keeping the organization alive. We keep on changing and developing as time demands because we want to make it grow continuously.

However, our perception of the word organization may be static. When we use the term in a business sense we look at something, which is final, done, not changing, a snapshot, a frame, or a photograph frozen in time. In reality, it is exactly the opposite because we are always in some changing system.

When we organize something, we do it to achieve something, a goal that we have in mind. Let us say we are in the business of selling pens. One person can sell 10 pens a day, so we decide to hire 10 people so that we can sell 100 pens in one day. We are organizing to make more money. This is a sales organization: organized to sell. As business grows more people are added and more money is made. More people however mean more costs in terms of salaries and more issues in terms of peoples' expectations etc. To manage these growing complexities we need finance/accounts people to manage money matters, HR people to manage the people issues and so forth. Hence, as complexities increase different types of 'organizations' spring up such as, in this example, a finance organization and a HR organization[*Ref.: Organization As a Garden*]. Now the overall organization consists of three distinct organizations.

This organization is given some structure because it helps us manage the growing complexities. So we may have a separate HR, finance, and marketing function with reporting relationships and career paths etc. This structure, which evolves in some hierarchical form, helps us manage the organization. However, a 'structure' we give to a certain situation, as in our example of an organization selling pens, is a temporary form of organization.

Suppose that over a period of time, personal selling is taken over by selling through the internet and all HR and finance related activities are outsourced because it is more cost effective. What will happen to the structure of yesteryears? Inevitably, it will change and a new structure will replace it, which may have just a few people with newer IT related skills running the core business. This is another move to manage complexities and change.

Merriam Webster Dictionary defines the word 'develop' as: to unfold gradually or in detail; to bring out the possibilities of; to make more available or usable; to acquire gradually; to go through a natural process of growth and differentiation (evolve); to become apparent. The same dictionary defines the word 'change' as: to make or become different (alter); to replace with another; the act, process, or result of changing.

The concept of organizing is closely linked with the concepts of developing and changing. Taking the example of our pen selling organization, as time goes on and more information becomes available the organization develops to cope with emerging complexities in order to achieve its objectives. Say that competitors launch a massive campaign with lowered prices and high advertising. Our company, hit by lowered sales, calls an emergency meeting in trying to cope with the new realities. In this meeting, it is discovered that the competition has a lower cost base to enable it to give such discounts. When this detail becomes available, our company has to generate options to compete with that. Say it does that by outsourcing its production and introducing newer and cheaper brands while retaining control over quality. It has developed, changed, and organized in a different way than before.

Hence organizing, developing and changing have two things in common: 1) they are all continuous in nature and 2) they all attempt to manage complexities. In other words, in order to achieve the desired results we organize to manage a maze of complexities in our operating environment and as the environment with its inherent complexities changes, we reorganize: develop & change. Life goes on.

EFFECTIVE ORGANIZATION

"All that spirits desire, spirits attain"-Khalil Gibran

Is there one best way to organize? Is the hierarchical organization a poorer version of the newer, leaner, meaner, process re-engineered organization? Are Self Directed Work Teams the rule rather than the exception? My answer is simply that you do what you have to do to get what you want. If this means living in a continuous state of flux then that is it and if it means a long period of maintaining the status quo than that is it. The real question here is what do you want and given your realities and aspirations, what are the best things to do? An effective organization would be one which takes into account the current realities and future aspirations.

HEAVY STUFF: VISION, PURPOSE ETC

"If you cease to dream you cease to exist"-Bible

Visions of grandeur must have become nauseating by now. Organizations who have caught the 'vision wave' have come up with many inspiring visions which, over time, are reduced to just graffiti. On the other hand, I believe, heart felt visions, shared visions, visions that people believe in and talk about catapult organizations to statures of greatness.

So what is vision? One of the best examples I can find is from the Black American movement led by Rev. [1]Martin Luther King Jr. His speech was his vision for his people, shared, believed, heartfelt and talked about. Here it is in full, it is worth it.

"I am very happy to join you today in what will go down in history as the greatest demonstration in the history of our nation. Five score years ago, a great American, in whose symbolic shadow we stand today, signed the Emancipation Proclamation. This momentous decree came as a great beacon light of hope to millions of Negro slaves, who had been seared in the flames of withering injustice. It came as a joyous daybreak to end the long night of their captivity.

But one hundred years later, the Negro is still not free. One hundred years later, the manacles of segregation and the chains of discrimination still sadly cripple the life of the Negro. One hundred years later, the negro lives on a lonely island of poverty in the midst of a vast ocean of material prosperity. One hundred years later, the Negro is still languished in the corners of American society and finds himself an exile in his own land. So we have come here today to dramatize a shameful condition.

In a sense we've come to our nation's capital to cash a check. When the architects of our republic wrote the magnificent words of the constitution and the Declaration of Independence, they were signing a promissory note to which every American was to fall heir. This note was a promise that all men-black men as well as white men-would be guaranteed the unalienable rights of life, liberty, and the pursuit of happiness.

It is obvious today that America has defaulted on this promissory note insofar as her citizens of color are concerned. Instead of honoring this sacred obligation, America has given the Negro people a bad check; a check, which has come back, marked 'insufficient funds'. But we refuse to believe that there are insufficient funds in the great vaults of this nation. So we've come to cash this check-a check, which will give us upon demand, the riches of freedom and the security of justice. We have also come to this hallowed spot to remind America of the fierce urgency of *now*. This is no time to engage in the luxury of cooling off or to take the tranquillizing drug of gradualism. Now is the time to make real the promise of democracy. Now is the time to rise from the dark and desolate valley of segregation to the sunlight of racial justice. Now is the time to lift our nation from the quicksand of racial injustice to the solid rock of brotherhood. Now is the time to make justice a reality of all God's children.

It would be fatal for the nation to overlook the urgency of the moment. This sweltering summer of the Negro's legitimate discontent will not pass until there is an invigorating autumn of freedom and equality. 1963 is not an end but a beginning. Those who hope that the Negro needed to blow off steam and will now be content will have a rude awakening if the nation returns to business as usual. There will be neither rest nor tranquility in America until the Negro is granted his citizenship rights. The whirlwinds of revolt will continue to shake the foundations of our nation until the bright day of justice emerges.

But there is something that I must say to my people who stand on the warm threshold, which leads into the palace of justice. In the process of gaining our rightful place we must not be guilty of wrongful deeds. Let us not seek to satisfy our thirst for freedom by drinking from the cup of bitterness and hatred.

We must forever conduct our struggle on the high plane of dignity and discipline. We must not allow our creative protest to degenerate into physical violence. Again and again we must rise to the majestic heights of meeting physical force with soul force. The marvelous new militancy which has engulfed the Negro community must not lead us to a distrust of all white people, for many of our white brothers, as evidenced by their presence here today, have come to realize that their freedom is inextricably bound to our freedom. We cannot walk alone.

And as we walk we must make the pledge that we shall always march ahead. We cannot turn back. There are those who ask the devotees of civil rights, 'When will you be satisfied?' We can never be satisfied as long as the Negro is the victim of the unspeakable horrors of police brutality. We can never be satisfied as long as our bodies, heavy with the fatigue of travel, cannot gain lodging in the motels of the highways and hotels of the cities. We cannot be satisfied as long as the Negro's basic mobility is from a smaller ghetto to a larger one. We can never be satisfied as long as our children are stripped from their selfhood and robbed of their dignity by signs stating 'For Whites Only.' We cannot be satisfied as long as a Negro in Mississippi cannot vote and a Negro in New York believes he has nothing for which to vote. No, no, we are not satisfied, and we will not be satisfied until justice rolls down like waters and righteousness like mighty stream.

I am not unmindful that some of you have come here out of great trials and tribulations. Some of you have come fresh from narrow jail cells. Some of you have come from areas where your quest for freedom left you battered by the storms of persecution and staggered by the winds of police brutality. You have been the veterans of creative suffering. Continue to work with the faith that unearned suffering is redemptive.

Go back to Mississippi, go back to Alabama, go back to South Carolina, go back to Georgia, go back to Louisiana, go back to the slums and ghettos of our northern cities knowing that somehow this situation can and will be changed. Let us not wallow in the valley of despair.

I say to you today, my friends, so even though we face the difficulties of today and tomorrow, I still have a dream. It is a dream deeply rooted in the American dream.

I have a dream that one day this nation will rise up and live out the true meaning of its creed: 'We hold these truths to be self-evident; that all men are created equal.'

I have a dream that one day on the red hills of Georgia the sons of former slaves and the sons of former slave owners will be able to sit down together at the table of brotherhood; I have a dream . . .

That one day even the state of Mississippi, a state sweltering with the heat of injustice, sweltering with the heat of oppression, will be transformed into an oasis of freedom and justice; I have a dream . . .

That my four little children will one day live in a nation where they will not be judged by the color of their skin but by the content of their character; I have a dream today.

I have a dream that one day in Alabama, with its vicious racists, with its governor having his lips dripping with the words of interposition and nullification, one day right there in Alabama little black boys and black girls will be able to join hands with little white boys and white girls as sisters and brothers; I have a dream today.

I have a dream that one day every valley shall be exalted, every hill and mountain shall be made low, and rough places will be made plain and crooked places will be made straight, and the glory of the Lord shall be revealed, and all flesh shall see it together.

This is our hope. This is the faith that I go back to the south with. With this faith we will be able to hew out of the mountain of despair a stone of hope. With this faith we will be able to transform the jangling discords of our nation into a beautiful symphony of brotherhood. With this faith we will be able to work together, to pray together, to struggle together, to go to jail together, to stand up for freedom together, knowing we will be free one day.

This will be the day . . . . This will be the day when all of God's children will be able to sing with new meaning 'My country 'tis of thee, sweet land of liberty, of thee I sing. Land where my fathers died, land of the pilgrim's pride, from every mountainside, let freedom ring,' and if America is to be a great nation—this must become true.

So let freedom ring—from the prodigious hilltops of New Hampshire, let freedom ring; from the mighty mountains of New York, let freedom ring—from the heightening Alleghenies of Pennsylvania!
Let freedom ring from the snowcapped Rockies of Colorado.
Let freedom ring from the curvaceous slopes of California!
But not only that; let freedom ring from the Stone Mountain of Georgia!
Let freedom ring from the Lookout Mountain of Tennessee!
Let freedom ring from every hill and molehill of Mississippi. From every mountainside let freedom ring, and when this happens . . . .

When we allow freedom to ring, when we let it ring from every village and every hamlet, from every state and every city, we will be able to speed up that day when all of God's children, black men and white men, Jews and Gentiles, Protestants and Catholics, will be able to join hands and sing in the words of the old Negro spiritual. **'Free at last! Free at last! Thank God Almighty, we are free at last.'"**

What would happen if the leaders of organizations would come up with dreams, which excite people and compel them to action? Why do organizational visions have to be one-liners? Why do we expect that one-liners will motivate people to give extra? Why can't we just speak our heart and let people make up their own versions and interpretations and share it in whichever way they like? I wonder.

So why don't we? Why do we leaders rely on gimmickry instead of focusing on the real issues: issues, which arise and fester deep inside our hearts? Issues which are bothering the people? Issues which have to be faced stark naked?

One plausible answer is that we really do not care. We may think and believe that we are here to make money and so is everyone else. This vision stuff is soft and even if it may be the 'in thing' nowadays, it is just talk, which is really, really, cheap! Eventually our thinking is translated into our actions and even if we say the lofty words, our actions betray us. One example that comes to mind is the misused phrase we have heard along the corridors of organizations, *"People are our most important assets . . . blah blah blah."* Yet when it comes down to it, they are the first to be released, let go or downsized rather 'right-sized'. If people are the most important asset of a company or if this is an organizational value written up everywhere for everyone to see, then in times of trouble letting go of your 'most important asset' should be the last option. In fact, fundamentally speaking, it should not be an option at all. Therefore, if people think that whatever you are giving them is just another variety of 'bull', it should not be surprising.

Another reason that leaders dodge the realities is perhaps fear. It could be fear of the unknown or it could be fear of facing up to the truth or both. Here I would like to quote a woman whom and whose work I admire and respect a lot, Christina Noble of Noble Foundation. She says, *"We cannot hope to bring about change unless we face the truth,"* of who we are, what we are, and where we are.

However, from the modern organizational perspective, does it really matter?

Eventually it boils down to making money and the more one makes the better the chances of survival. So where do vision, purpose and values fit in? Rather how do they provide an edge if all organizations have them, how do they compete? Probably the best answer, as I've come across, is found in Jim Collins' masterpiece, Built To Last[2]. The core message is that organizations need to be 'genuine.'

Mr. Collins and his team talk about myths, like the most successful companies exist to maximize profits. They explain that visionary companies are guided by a core ideology, core values, and a sense of purpose beyond just making money. Moreover, that these core values seldom change if at all. Strategies and goals are changed without compromising their cherished core ideals. Another myth: Companies become visionary primarily through vision statements. The truth Collins & Co., have found is that great companies build mechanisms to achieve the vision through consistent hard work and dedication. The oft-quoted 3M example of 'Post It Notes' is a case in point.

WHAT IS IT REALLY & WHY DOES IT MATTER?

In today's war torn world everyone, or at least some of us, are 'fighting for peace' and they are fighting with armed weapons. However, they will not find it as we all know because peace is found within the hearts. Therefore, their efforts are doomed to failure. This is also the difference between what we say and what we do; the lower the difference, the higher the integrity.

I'm reminded of a Sufi anecdote of Mullah Nassruddin. Once he was looking for something under the street light. Some passersby inquired if he had lost something. To which he replied 'yes I've lost my keys.' The passersby asked, 'is it here that you lost them?' 'No, I lost them near my door.' Mullah replied. Surprised, the passersby asked, 'So why are you looking for them here?' to which the Mullah replied, 'Because it is dark over there!' The message: being genuine with what you envision the organization to be and achieve; face the issues as they are instead of pushing them down the carpet and saying everything is fine. Speaking lofty words and taking crude actions is like looking for the keys in the wrong place. If one is sincere with the vision, it takes real hard work, which is like looking for the keys exactly where they were lost, in the dark.

In other words, visions help save the organizations in times of trouble. When the chips are down it is the drive and energy, which forces people to come out and above the adversities. Therefore, it matters because it gives people something to aim for. Additionally, people only strive to achieve that vision, which they feel, has been communicated not as eyewash, or something with which the leaders themselves do not seem sincere. As far as it is genuine, it regulates the peoples' behavior as they deal with seemingly unrelated issues and manage to deal with them.

The usual practice is that after making a vision statement one goes on to defining mission statement and then forms SMART objectives and so on. In my view, one should move to mechanisms for achieving the vision right after finalizing and agreeing to the vision. These mechanisms, once in place, will then lead to the objectives, which will then lead to the strategies a company may employ to achieve them.

Say you envision becoming the world's best Hollywood star. What would make more sense talking about the short-term mission of say getting the right agent or thinking about putting in place such mechanisms whereby you can achieve your longer-term goal? While getting an agent is not something you can miss, you also would need to take steps to ensure your long-term success. For example, you can start by asking what would make you the best. This would probably require good acting skills, so you need to take some lessons and keep on taking other related trainings to keep you on your toes. You would probably require to be very self critical, examine the work you do and identify areas for improvement. Perhaps you can start associating with people, even if they are your staunchest critics, whose opinions you can trust or at least mull over. You can also study the actors you think are the best and try to figure out what makes them so good, and so forth. These individual habits, mechanisms, are the key to your becoming the best and achieving your dream.

26/11/01

'Time flies. I joined in April and its November, wow! I guess one could call it the game of survival. Let us see what is in store for me now. Somehow I feel that there is a difference between me and the other managers, they tend to stick together leaving me alone. Well, never mind, I must focus on my life, my goals, and my ambitions. Let's hope that my Master will have planned the best for me and I must go with His plans . . .'

THE HOW PART: STRATEGY

"All men can see the tactics whereby I conquer, but what none can see is the strategy out of which great victory is evolved."—Sun-Tzu

Now suppose that our company, in the sports market, Pro Inc. has the following dream: *'To be the first choice of every athlete in the country.'* How would it go about achieving this dream? The first obvious step would be to work out a long-term strategy. How does it want to make money? And how does it want to position itself and its brands?

THE EXTERNAL ENVIRONMENT

Let us say it has three major brands to start with: **Elite** its elite class, up market, expensive brand; **Premier** its medium class version, closely following the lines of the elite class brand; and **Classics** the mass appeal, lower priced, college student version. Let us also assume that Pro Inc. has its own manufacturing facilities and distributes its products through a nation wide network of distributors and wholesalers.

The economy has been sluggish for quite some time and it has been suggested that in the days to come, as competition increases, many local businesses will flounder because the imported products will be cheaper and are reputed to be of high quality. Currently Pro Inc. faces stiff competition from only one other local company Jerker Inc. whose low category, mass appeal brand **Harker** has consistently won out over **Classics**. **Elite** and **Premier** do not feel that pressure from any other Jerker brand but have been bothered quite a lot by counterfeit brands, legally imported brands and smuggled brands. While they dominate share of the market, it has been getting difficult to sustain that position. Jerker Inc. on the other hand, deals mostly in lower end brands and competes on the basis of price, hence it is not that affected by neither **Elite** nor by **Premier's** performances because the consumers for these are different than **Harker** and other lower brands.

Given this imaginary situation, what is Pro Inc. to do? Somehow, the leadership of the company has to translate its vision into reality. What does being the first choice for every athlete in the country mean? Etc.

ELITE

For **Elite** the user looks for status symbol. The user belongs to a high-income group and prefers quality to price. Quality is defined as comfort and style. The price range can be anything comparable to all international brands. On the other hand, when it comes to competition from international brands the local cost base is much higher because of the smaller market size and lower production volumes. The counterfeit products being made by the same name create an image issue because of their poor quality standards, and their reach, which is almost comparable because they use the same distribution channels, especially the wholesale. Their success is due to the higher margins *(almost up by 30%)* they give to the trade channels *(from distributors to wholesalers to retailers)*.

PREMIER

Premier enjoys a unique position in the market as well. It is not as expensive as Elite and it follows the same design lines although customized for a younger generation. It is fresh yet professional, hip yet sober and stylish and yet usable. It is also just as comparable to any international brand but at the same time stands to lose the most once the market becomes open for competition. This is so because the competitors are also very focused on this lucrative segment and their cost bases are extremely low which enables them to offer the same quality at much lower price. Counterfeit and smuggling sector is also very keen on this particular market segment because it not only gives high margins but also high volumes. It is mildly price sensitive.

CLASSIC

Classic products are for the masses, and make up the most volume in terms of units for the company. It is very popular with the students of all ages and its price is low enough, although highly sensitive to price changes as well, to generate demand in this segment. It's hip and fashionable but more colorful, zesty and extremely stylish. It is also here that Harker gives it tough competition, especially because Jerker Inc. specializes in low priced high fashion products and Harker is its top line and there are three more brands below that price range. This enables Jerker to command a larger market share overall in this price sector. It does that because of its lower cost base and very large production volume. It also gives better margins to the trade channels which makes it a favorite for the distributors, wholesalers and retailers.

FOOD FOR THOUGHT FOR LEADERS

Put yourself in the shoes of the top management of Pro Inc. Where would you start? What would you do? In normal everyday organizational lives, these kinds of scenarios are always present in one way or another. Our managers are always busy tackling these issues; that is the reason why they are there in the first place. So what do they normally do? This is a question, which perhaps you can answer best.

As managers, have you ever questioned what exactly were you hired to do? If you are thinking about your job description, you are dead wrong! The answer is simply that you were hired to use the best of your abilities to make the organization effective. Your job description only limits your endeavors to a certain frame of reference, and that too for a certain period of time. As you progress from one grade to another or from one project to another or from one position to another, your frame of reference changes. What does not change over a period of time is your real job: 'to make the organization effective'. That is why HR's role in coming up with realistic and to the point job/role descriptions is ever more important. Similarly, one can do the real job of making the organization more effective only if one believes in the vision as something to strive for, wholeheartedly. Unfortunately, it is not as cut and dried as it sounds.

29/11/01

'This month is about to end, so is this year. About 32 days left for 2002 to start. Time flies when you are having fun, or even when you are not. I have bided my time here and now increasingly I feel that I need to move on. Nothing left to do here. There is nothing much I can do for myself here. Every single person in this organization is fed up and they come up with all sorts of ways to compensate for their loss of ego, self-esteem, and self-respect. Pathetic management. What a pity!'

SPIRALS OF INVOLVEMENT

Organizations create, what I call, "Spirals of Involvement." As a manager one keeps swirling around in these spirals, with no time to look around, as managers, we tend to lose track of our original direction. It's like sightseeing on our way to a certain destination. We get so caught up in the scenery; we forget why we ever set foot out. Was it because of the scenic views? I hope not. As a manager, what was it that we were supposed to do? Why did we join? Why were we hired?

In my observation, most managers as they become 'managers' do not know the answer to the question 'why are we here?' Instead of making their organization effective, they focus on getting ahead in the company, regardless of what it takes. They just do or 'manage' whatever comes their way and what does come their way are usually and seemingly isolated and unrelated problems and issues. These managers simply manage these issues, big or small, related to people or systems, not ever looking at the big picture if it does not relate to their promotion or pay raise or mere existence.

That is why I became a manager, to find out what is so pervasive in organizations that makes people lose their original spirit, if you will, and become cogs in a wheel, waiting for the next promotion.

On the contrary, I've also experienced moments where a manager's concern about the big picture, his 'questioning' of the current organizational realities and his feedback to his senior managers about the things that are going wrong or his suggestions for improvement, have been critically looked down upon. What is a manager, a leader in this case, supposed to think and do? On facing an instance like that and discussing it with a friend, I was told: 'No one likes to hear the truth. This is not how organizations work. It's not about truth; it's about keeping the job!' And that, in my opinion, is the problem.

An organization that rewards individual performance rather than team performance creates a spiral where everyone is forced to think about himself/herself. An organization which works on the premises of MBO (managing by objectives), in my view, may fall into the trap of short sightedness, as objectives have a tendency to 'de-link' themselves from the overall vision of an organization. In the pursuit of individual results and short-term objectives, managers may take the trees for the forest. They may become very good at cutting down trees to make way, achieving objectives, but seldom question if they are moving in the right direction.

First Ring Down the Spiral

When managers are confronted with problems and ensuing decisions that they make or have to make, they usually do not consider the big picture. The seemingly 'un-relatedness' of the issues that come across, makes each manager decide without considering the effects any particular decision may have overall. So decisions in marketing may be made in isolation of HR or production and vice versa. Moreover, all decision may be made in light of the specific objectives and not the vision.

Second Ring Down the Spiral

Since it's 'every man for himself", there is an environment of competition. Hence, everyone is caught up in trying to come out as a winner. Eventually not everyone can be given that sought after title and only a handful move forward. The drive to win can push people to get involved in areas of political maneuvering which they should not be involved in to begin with. However, what politics a person plays varies from person to person and really, depends on his/her intentions.

In short, whatever spirals of involvement an organization creates, managers 'have to get' caught up in these if they are to survive. They make their own survival strategies some focusing on getting the work done and being extremely good at it. Some do it by harnessing good relationships with their bosses and so forth. A manager who thinks like a leader will tend to stop these spirals dead in their tracks and rise above them. A leader who thinks like a manager will tend to get better at working within these spirals and getting into them deeper and deeper.

MOVING UP THE SPIRALS-STEP 1

In my experience of being a manager I have seen that values, living according to these values, and acting on them is the only way one can avoid going down these spirals. All it takes is for one to stick to his/her values, principles and morals. All decisions, if weighed against these values, will take the organization and the people within this organization in the right direction. Whether these are organizational values or personal, consistency of action (Integrity, as it is called) according to these values is the answer.

MOVING UP THE SPIRAL-STEP 2

If a manager's role is to make his/her organization effective, how is he/she to do that? The answer lies in realizing that 'a manager' cannot be responsible for delivering the results. He/she is only responsible in ensuring that his/her team is enabled to deliver results. Hence, the focus needs to be on the development of the team, the frontline soldiers, and a manager's accountability lies in his/her ability to create a high performing team.

This incidentally reminds of a very funny story someone forwarded to me via email[3] it is called:

"Corporate Donkeys"

"Donkeys are collectively an essential driving force of many organizations. Sounds like a preposterous comment? The idea is neither to insult the donkeys or the organizations, but to comment on the phenomenon that has quietly crept into our corporate system. The donkeys I am referring to are human in structure, but have key personality traits, which are found in donkeys (or asses, if you choose to call them that). Hence, going by cerebral nexus, they are closer to donkeys than to humans. In any case, one should not be deceived by looks alone *(such as cases where vixens are confused with women)*.

Now, the donkeys that I am talking about are handy commodities for any institutions. When they are assigned a job, they obediently respond and without asking any questions, set about doing their task. They work head down, from dusk till dawn everyday. Hard work is their forte, and not much else. Since they are donkeys by character, they are known to either possess the least of expectations, especially of any immediate monetary reward, or have a wealth of patience to wait for these remunerations. This realization is not lost on the organization and they make full use of the donkeys since such cheap bonded labor is hard to find elsewhere.

However, these donkeys have one common trait running across the whole community. They believe that since they have worked so untiringly, outperforming others, they have earned great management respect. They harbor the illusion that the management is deeply impressed and has higher things in store for them in the long run. For this precise false thinking and nothing more, these livings forms should be called donkeys. The secret is that the management has beaten them in the competition of the discovery of their race. Self-awakening in any way is usually hard to come by. The management, therefore, does not believe in elevating the donkeys, as they are aware of their innate capacity to survive on low sustenance.

The question that might bother some of us is that being a donkey means being a paragon of dumbness. Then how come they are able to do so much complex work. Well, their dumbness is not related to performance, but based on the fact that they fail to realize that: a) consistent hard work is the surest way to let the bosses decipher your race; b) moving up the ladder requires things other than hard work.

These donkeys need to redefine their role in society or at least in the organization. The biggest problem is self-realization. Therefore, I suggest that every employee should take stock and establish whether he is a donkey or otherwise. Certain measures can then be adopted to de-donkey oneself at his/her convenience *(mind you, it is much difficult than de-toxicating)*. First of all, one should be prepared to accept the bitter reality and should not feel any shame if the end result labels one as a donkey. After all, you would be discovering something, which has been common knowledge for the management for many years. The following are some simple steps of a self-administered *test (aptly called the Road to Self Discovery or RSD)* that can lead to the classification of corporate employees into humans and donkeys. For classification such as owls, grasshoppers and butterflies, readers should await future articles in this genre.

The R.S.D. Test

- You regularly forget to call your wife even once in a day due to work pressure.
- You are expecting a promotion and a new company-maintained car in the next six months, for the last five years.
- You are the only one who has not taken a vacation this year.
- In the morning, you keep the newspaper aside, thinking that first some work on the desk should be disposed of. The paperboy eventually collects 30 unread newspapers at the end of the month from your desk.
- Each evening, you have to return the wish 'see you tomorrow' uttered by every single staff member to you.
- You become a routine OW carrier to your home. OW stands for office work and not a sexual disease.
- Every odd year, your eyesight sheds a digit and your headache refuses to leave you in peace.
- Your promotion and privileges are denied on the basis of some clerical objections.

If the answers to all the points above are 'yes' then the diagnosis is that you are a donkey without being aware of this somewhat humiliating reality.

The following steps are advisable: Focus your concentration on the social activities of the organization or to put it bluntly, of your top bosses. Intrude in seminars attended by your bosses, followed by parties attended by your superiors. More appropriate are those prestigious balls. Booking tables in those balls is highly recommended and is a proven way to succeed professionally.

Socializing and being perceived as a social animal is the key to corporate success in the land of the pure.

Play the game of the management. You must find the donkey-like subordinates in your midst who should be bucked up and encouraged to take up additional work and responsibility. They will serve as your proxy. Hand this article to them once they are transferred and no longer working for you. Finally, you will find that activities outside the office pay greater dividends. This is the key area that was being neglected before. If you are awarded your promotion in the next six months, it means that you are an improved race now! Occasional re-reading of this article is recommended ☺

(While I do not agree with everything suggested in this fine article, some concepts are really worth thinking about.)

MARKET DYNAMICS

Recently the management of Pro Inc. had received indications that a multinational company, Dominant Brands International (**DBI**), might be entering their market soon. DBI had recently conducted a test market of one of their high-end brands. Although the results hadn't been impressive, the Pro Inc management fears that once they come in with their full blown portfolio, it could be quite disastrous for the existing market dominance of Pro Inc. Plus the fact that they used Jerker Inc. as 'test partners' is also not a very encouraging sign for Pro Inc. This multinational is the international market leader with very deep pockets. This had send shivers down the spine of many and Many are awaiting this arrival anxiously because they see possible career moves. because they see a possible career moves. The board meeting which was hurriedly convened at this point left the marketing director with the responsibility of finding out what this new competition would mean for the company and what should their strategy be.

The marketing director arranged a daylong brainstorming session to make sense of all the information. This session, which was attended by all the marketing officials and people from finance, product development, and production, was very useful. Here is its summary:

The first step was to conduct a comparative SWOT for Pro Inc., and DBI (The potential new competitor). The results were as follows:

Pro Inc.'s strengths lie in a strong market presence, especially in the high & premium sector. It leads the industry at home with a strong brand portfolio. DBI on the other hand, has a strong corporate and brand image and it is the international leader in this industry. Pro Inc.'s weakness was identified as having a lack of clear direction, as it tried to play all segments of the market. DBI's weakness on the other hand was identified as entering a mature market with a very strong brand affiliation. The threat to Pro Inc. was seen to be DBI's partnership with Jerker Inc., whereby it could sweep the market from both ends, squeezing Pro Inc. in the middle. The threat to DBI was identified as adapting to the local markets and cultural acceptance. The opportunities lying ahead for Pro Inc. seem to be to achieve economies of scale to an extent whereby it could produce products at half the cost of its competition.

Various scenarios were also developed which were combined to form one likely scenario that the competition would adopt to enter Pro Inc.'s market. Here is what it looked like:

"DBI has entered the market focusing on the market shared between Elite and Premier. They have introduced their international brands at par with these two brands, pricing them at the same price points, giving the customers a very good value for money, since these brands drive much higher prices internationally. Their partnership with Jerker Inc. has given extra boost to the competition, which is now investing very heavily in its mass volume brands like Harker. This has greatly troubled Classics' sales. DBI is using Jerker Inc.'s distribution network but has hired a separate field force, which is very highly trained and paid. This has also hurt Pro Inc. because many of its bright managers have shifted over. DBI operates from a nearby port city, importing its brands from there. This gives them additional flexibility as they can command lower costs and lower commitment in terms of infrastructure setup and oversee a larger market. Already Pro Inc.'s leadership is faltering and it seems that 'we might not last for more than three years, unless we can bring our costs down dramatically!'"

The scenario had sent shivers down the marketing director's spine! What strategy could Pro Inc. adopt to counter this impending threat of extinction?

THIS IS OUR PYRAMID: STRUCTURE

"Structures of which we are unaware hold us prisoner." Peter Senge

Before we move on, let's also consider the internal environment. How is our company geared up to face the challenges of the future? Is it structured to give quick customer service, is it flexible or bureaucratic? Etc.

THE INTERNAL ENVIRONMENT

Suppose that our company Pro Inc. has evolved over a period, as a hierarchical, traditional pyramid organization. The various functions have grown in fiefdoms, which include marketing, HR, production, finance, IT, and corporate & legal affairs department. Each has a functional director, which makes them a team of five as they all report to the old man who looks after the corporate & legal affairs department himself. He is also the founder and CEO, is 70 years of age, and going strong!

The old man had always believed in professionalism and hence has included prominent business personalities in the company's non-executive board. Some of his family members are working in the company, but are subject to the system like everyone else. The VPs are all home grown except for the VP IT, who is also younger, 38 years old, in comparison to the average age of 50.

There are three factories with 900 workers, out of which approximately three quarters are skilled and they are all controlled by a team of managers.

This team includes the Factory Manager (FM Manager), HR Manager, Industrial Relations Manager, Technical Training & Development Manager, Production Managers, Factory Engineer, Maintenance Manager, Finance Manager, and the Security Manager. The FM reports to the VP Production while the other managers report directly to him. HR & IR managers have dotted line relationship with the VP HR, and similarly the Financial Services Manager reports to the VP Finance, Factory Engineer to the Chief Engineer etc.

At the head office, which is geographically situated in the middle of these three factories, the VPs sit with the rest of their entourage. T&D, remuneration, recruitment, payments, buying, corporate communication etc, are all centralized processes. All targets and budgets are approved at the head office by the board of directors.

The brands are also managed from the head office by the brand management group that report in to the head of brands who reports to the VP Marketing. Similarly, head of sales who reports to the VP Marketing as well heads the sales team, spread through out the country. From a sales perspective, the country is divided into 5 regions overseen by regional managers who report to the head of sales. Each region in turn is divided into areas according to the potential sales volume, overseen by area managers who report in to the regions. The sales team is 150 strong.

To provide faster and better services, the finance department is divided into various sections. One is looking after the financial concerns of operations and another to look after marketing. Then there is the corporate finance section, which is responsible for collating all the financial results and takes care of corporate accounting. HR & IT are the support departments facilitating smooth flow of various organizational processes.

The organizational pyramid looks something like this:

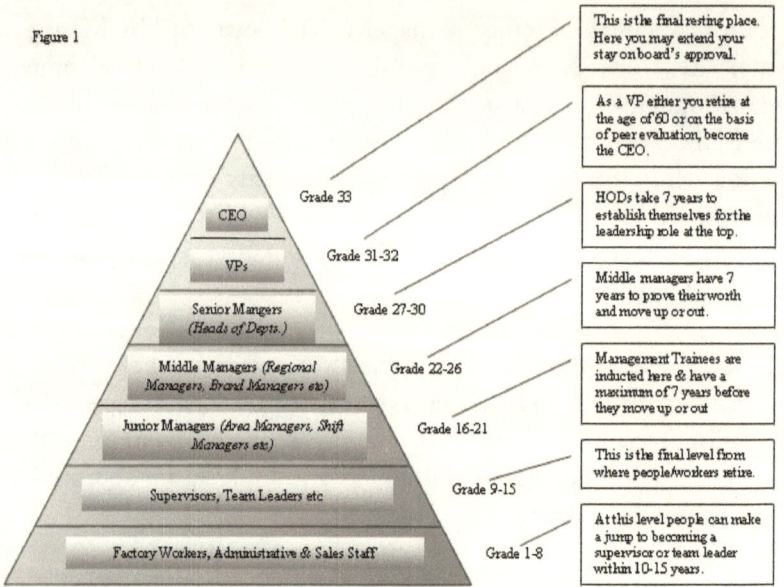

Figure 1

The management trainees are hired at the age of 25, which means that everyone has a 35 year-window of reaching the top spot, and that is the basis of all competition internally. People are also hired laterally in various levels apart from the trainee level. At the junior management level, everyone has a chance of being promoted five times in 7 years. That is the standard. Similarly, at the middle management level one has a chance of being promoted four times in another 7 years. At the senior management level, there is a chance of being promoted three times in 7 years. At the VP level, one can hope for two promotions in 7 years. Finally, as the CEO, one has seven years to contribute.

THE PECKING ORDER

"To be in hell is to drift; to be in heaven is to steer." George Bernard Shaw

Every kind of pecking order has its own pros and cons. Pyramids have this problem: very few people make it to the top. This implies a consistent tussle amongst the hopefuls of the next promotion. While this competition is healthy insofar as it encourages extra efforts in given job parameters, it is also unhealthy because it is the basis of de-motivation as well. Suppose two managers are eyeing the next slot and both of them are equally capable and have the potential etc. Only one makes it. What would the other one feel? Maybe out of frustration he would resign and go to the competitor or he can decide to be devious and stay and try to make his employees' life a living hell and so forth.

For Pro Inc., this happens to be a major dilemma. Many of its bright performers from marketing, finance, production etc., have been leaving the company over the past three years. All of these have been from the middle management *(which means a minimum of 5 years of experience and training down the drain)*. The most common reason cited for this problem has been termed 'lack of growth'. Majority of people have left to go to other industries and some even to the competitor. The most common HR response to this so far has been to hire new ones and to shuffle around the existing staff by creating new positions and roles, proudly calling it re-structuring.

Not realizing that the talent, which is leaving, takes at least three to five years to replace, the HR has usually quoted that the average turnover of employees in the country is 3% where as Pro Inc. stands at 1.95%. In the words of the HR director, *'with the given market situation where jobs are already very hard to find, where unemployment rate is a staggering 14%, we have nothing to worry about.'* This has not satisfied many concerned employees of the company. The grapevine has it that HR is doing nothing but keeping records, but no one confronts the HR director simply because of his relationship with the CEO. In fact, the whole department is an element of fear in the entire company.

Recently the HR department had appointed an outside OD consultant to study the organization and suggest improvements. The report had made the HR department look incompetent, which had infuriated the HR team. The major finding had been that the HR department is still acting as the personnel department of yesteryears. There are still HR managers in the company who think that HR is all about labor laws and union negotiations. However, interestingly, even if that was the case, they are doing a poor job, especially when it comes to the long-term consequences of all decisions. Talk about blunt report writing!

Decision making, on the other hand, is slow. This is not just limited to HR, but seems to be an organizational issue. Each decision, whether it is about hiring someone, launching a new product, or reacting to some competitor action has to go through a number of bureaucratic channels, up and down the hierarchy, before it can be finalized and implemented. Over the past five years, with the increasing pace of business and introduction of newer technology, the slow decision-making has become a very weak point for the organization. The general feeling is that every day the time drags on and on and yet work never seems to be finished. Meetings, and more meetings; reports and reviewed report; work and re-work and the same thing day in and day out. People seem to be losing sleep, hair, and health faster than in any other company.

The consultant had been courageous to point out that making the wrong decision is not an issue. In her views, if a decision is made, it must be assumed that it is made keeping the interests of the organization in clear view. It is just that sometimes the circumstances surrounding the decision favor it and sometimes they do not, in which case it is called a mistake or a wrong decision. Her point of view is that the problem lies in the 'watering down' of the decision's impact. In other words, it is the 'risk averse attitude' of the managers, which turns every decision into a tedious round of table talks.

Career Management has also come out as a major weakness in the overall dissatisfaction in the company's culture. There is no on going environmental analysis, no estimation of exact manpower requirements with the evolving future, no development plan for the staff as per their knowledge, skills and attitude profile, no retention strategy or policy, no succession planning, and no strategy for maintaining motivation among the employed. In fact, HR is NOT acting as a strategic partner in the growth and business development of the organization. [*Ref.:* **Human Resource Planning**]

The consultant had also laid a lot of emphasis on Training & Development in the company and here are some views from her personal diary:

"The role of T&D is simply to increase organizational effectiveness, pure and simple. It is not about budget fulfillment or the head count in terms of covering the maximum number of people or optimum man-hours of training spent. These are all by products or measuring tools of how much quantitative value T&D has added in organization. Most managers when they read this would probably think that it is just bullshit. They are right from their point of view. Many organizations rarely understand that actual T&D contribution lies in the bottom line performance. People rarely understand that this training in EI (emotional intelligence) or NLP (neuro-linguistic programming) is beneficial. This is a two-way thing.

The training manager's responsibility lies in being able to give training within the budget. She examines the needs through the performance appraisal process and tries to give the required service by finding appropriate courses for the 'would be' candidates. This is pretty simple and pretty boring. It requires little creativity or ingenuity. It also adds no value. That is why training budgets are the first to go, when the going gets tough.

Employees find, to their disliking, when they are sent on a course they know that they know 'only too well'. Functional/technical training they can live with because it will directly affect their performance on the job. It will make them look good to their line managers, as an added advantage. *"But who cares about creative problem solving? Isn't that something we already know and use?"* Hence such courses are treated with indifference at the least and 'enjoyment' at best. No link is established to real work life, where problems come as a daily surprise. *"Who has the time to do the force field analysis when the union is riding our ass? And who's keeping the score anyway?"*

Can we see the missing link yet?

If ever we needed OD interventions internally, it is in the T&D department and more specifically in the T&D approach towards organizational effectiveness.

Real value addition from T&D is in qualitative aspects. Obviously, hard-nosed executives and managers can rarely see this. What is more interesting is when the senior HR manager or director or worse, the CEO, proclaims that we are in the business of making money. In addition, if we are not making money than there is no use in investing in training and all other developmental activities. Actually, they are on the other side of the tunnel. A good question to ask now would be that if we were not doing so well, then what do we need to do to reverse the situation? One answer could be to push harder, work harder and earn those dollars. I, on the other hand, say that we need to invest in our people in a way that enables them to achieve the targets that they have been missing. This is about aligning the T&D activities with business goals, and keeping a track of them. So long as T&D is linked with bottom line, is shown in the respective job profile, and is measured in the performance appraisal process, it will be done.

Before a real war is fought, days and months are spent in training the troops for the event. Training is given for any eventuality. It is thorough and becomes second nature for those who qualify. In the end, when it comes down to it, this is what saves lives. Why doesn't the same principle apply to business settings? In business settings, people just jump in, as if they know it all. Business schools provide the functional backgrounds through various teaching methods, which, if nothing else, gives people theoretical grounding. This is the knowledge part of it. For skills, various training programs either in-house or outsourced are used by various organizations. However, what is lacking is that readiness or preparation which is given in the army. While I do not want organizations to consider or to function as an army, I do admit that I am more impressed with their approach towards training." [*Ref.: The Role of T & D*]

04/12/01

'It's a good thing I write my thoughts. It helps me deal with the daily pressures of working here. I think time has now come to open up and confront the issues upfront whatever the results maybe. I must stand up for what I believe in. I must give feedback on specific and quotable incidents that led me to lose my cool. If no one would tell them, they will never know. Henceforth, if this attitude takes me out of this miserable shit hole, I will happily go. At least I will have the guts to stand up for what I believe in. I believe this is the way it should have been from the start, but better late than never.'

THE 'INSEPARABILITY' OF THEORY & PRACTICE

"When someone says he is a practical man, what he means is that he is using old fashioned theories." A Cynic

The issues of structure are about the basic human urge to control. This control of how the organization behaves *(how the people in the organization behave collectively)* in various environments is necessary for its efficient functioning *(achieving its objectives)*. Over the past one century, much attention has been given to this subject.

What sort of structure is best for any given organization with its given objectives and a way of doing business?

A very long time ago, when I was a kid I watched a black & white Disney movie about a horse. He was a good horse who had a good master. His master believed in taking good care of his animal. He fed him well and gave him of his love and care. Slowly, with practice, the horse started winning races. The master was very happy and gave more of his love to the horse. Then he had to sell this horse. The new master was quite opposite in character. He wanted the horse to win all the time because he wanted to make more money. His set up was more professional, where there was no room for personal care and touch, but just mechanical routines. The horse missed his old master and the attention he got from him. Not getting that the horse lost a race. In return, the new master was harsh to him and reduced his feed. The horse got weaker, lost another race. His feed was reduced again. This started a vicious circle, until the horse was so feeble that he could barely walk. At that time, he was let go. Fortunately, for little kids like us, this story had a happy ending. His old master found him and took care of him, and the horse was happy and strong again, a winning horse that he had always been!

Douglas McGregor gave a striking parallel in management theory with his theory X *(first let them win then feed them)* and theory Y *(first feed them then let them win)*. The story is the same. Whether you believe in theory x or y, it affects how you manage within an organization. Whatever your theory, it will be translated into your policies and systems you adopt for managing the organization. This in turn will structure your organization, which will influence how people behave in such an environment.

As with Pro Inc., it started out with a small selling outfit and slowly grew into a big company with manufacturing facilities etc. In the beginning, things were simple as most employees reported directly to the founder. As the size grew, complexities increased and more structures and systems were put in place to manage these complexities. This is the usual story behind almost every organization since no one in the infancy periods actually sits down and designs the organization to grow in a certain way. The principle of hierarchy and the ensuing command and control system is just a natural outgrowth of increasing complexity simply because it is common sense.

All organizations I can think of work in some form of theory X with some variations on theory Y. This perhaps has to do with the natural mistrust we have of all other humans around us. We pay people after they have worked for a month because we want to, first, get the work out of them. Why do we not pay them before we get the work out of them? Possibly, because we think it is unsafe and unwise. In essence then, what we say to our employees from the very start is '*We don't trust you buggers, but you must trust "us"*'. Unfortunately, however, this is how the world seems to be structured.

Common sense suggests that there must be someone responsible enough to supervise a bunch of people so that we can have our peace of mind. Moreover, if things go not quite as we plan, we can give that one person our piece of mind. Therefore, the hierarchy develops from top to bottom or vice versa. This hierarchy can be bureaucratic in nature with lots of standard operating procedures, which regulate how work needs to be done. It does not really matter whether this hierarchy has four levels or fourteen; the urge to control how work is done will make it a command and control system, which will be bureaucratic in nature.

Bureaucracy by nature makes decision making slow because it has to go through a certain number of channels for the purposes of accountability and control. It is also about centralization of power. If one wants to have the power to decide about anything, one really wants to control. With such a personality, this person, perhaps a control freak, does not expect that anyone else would be able to make a prudent decision on his behalf. That is also taking things very personally, which, by the way, is very non-bureaucratic by definition. Hence, it is not so much the requirement of having a command and control system in an organization, which makes me want to puke. It is the attitude of people within this system, which is infuriating. In essence, these people make other people feel trivialized and make all their abilities and education simply come to naught, by one stroke of the pen.

Hierarchical or pyramid organizations are rather common in the business world because they are the way things have developed over almost a thousand years. Perhaps it started with the first conscious family roles differentiation based on physical power and mental inabilities. It is however, sad that many organizations still follow this same ancient principle. There are many other forms of organizations available and many others 'can be created' if one were only to think about it.

SYSTEMS: THE ENGINES OF GROWTH & SUSTAINABILITY

"In order to discover new lands, one must be willing to lose sight of the shore for a very long time." Anonymous

Systems are probably the most important aspect of managing people within an organization. Whether it is the career management system, the performance management system, or any other system, its quality and appropriateness to the organizational environment and vision is paramount. It is about how things get done. The more effective the systems are the more effective the organization is.

Organization, as I have said before, is how people gather together to achieve something. Whether it is a soccer team or cricket team, people have been organized to achieve victory. Hence, when we talk about success or failure, we are talking about how effective or ineffective this organization has been. Although, it would be incomplete without talking about the individuals within this organization, for the time being we will focus on managing this organized body.

For Pro Inc.'s vision of becoming the preferred choice, its current reality and future aspirations, and the strategies to cope with the reality and achieve its goals, it needs to come up with systems that guarantee its success for the future. Let us look at how this pyramid organization's systems currently work.

Career management and performance management systems are geared to ensure that only the best of the best rise to the top. Hence, the seniors, particularly in the HR department, are paternalistic in their approach towards the rising stars. Since the top slots are few and the candidates are plenty, the backbone of the two processes rests on critical evaluations. How well one is doing, and how far can one go are the two most important considerations in this setup.

On the other side of the coin, however, the people feel that the two systems are flawed, as they are too subjective. This raises the question of favoritism. Anyone who is closer to her line manager seems to get the next promotion and anyone who is blunt and truthful seems to stay down. People complain bitterly that performance is not the only criteria of promotion. Another thing that bothers people is the HR department's assertion about the ultimate potential of any employee. This is the basis on which it is decided who goes how far up in the pyramid. People have many issues with this idea as well and do not approve of the thinking at all.

Respective line managers do the Performance Appraisal (PA) once every year. It is based on last year's goals and targets. The process is as follows:

At the beginning of the year, targets are set whether they be production targets, quality targets, sales targets etc. In order to achieve these targets the directors sit down and work out how their departments are going to contribute. Then these are further cascaded downwards to all the people working within that department and they work out how they are going to help achieve these targets. Once the year has ended, each line manager sits down to assess how close the people have come to achieving their targets. This process is repeated year after year for all the managers. Based on what ratings a person gets in his or her PA, which is given to him/her by the line manager, his/her annual bonus/increment is decided.

In order to assess the training needs of individuals, another sort of appraisal is conducted simultaneously. This appraisal is called Development Review (DR). It is closely linked with the PA process. The assumption behind this DR is that if a person is not able to achieve 100% of the goals and targets given to him then there is something lacking in this person. What is lacking in this person and what sort of activities would be required to fill that gap in a reviewer's assessment is what DR produces. Based on these PA/DR processes, the 'reviewed' not only gets the increment but also his/her development activities are established which are to be fulfilled over the course of next year.

Recently, the management of Pro Inc. has started another process called 360° feedback, whereby the reviewed have been given this freedom to discuss their ratings with their line managers/reviewers. It has been done because the management has felt after a long time that the reviewed have a right to defend their performances and that the PA/DR process needs to be a two-way communication. However, lack of proper training on how to work with 360° feedback has created another set of problems.

The second system for people management is the Career Tracking System or CTS. This is purely HR's baby. Supported by an information system, which carries all the information regarding all the managers of the company from grade 16 upwards, the CTS is used to manage and advise managers on how their career is going. The CTS is based on a career management model the company has adopted. This model stipulates the rules governing the career growth of managers.

One stipulation of this model is that everyone at any grade has to spend a certain amount of time before she can be considered for a promotion. For instance, if one is hired at grade 16 in the marketing department, that person has to perform at various designations within the department for sometime before she can be promoted to grade 17. In addition, to move from this frontline or junior management level, a person must have worked for a maximum of seven years in various roles before she moves on to grade 22.

As the nature of the funnel suggests, as one moves up the hierarchy, the promotions start becoming rare. Hence, the competition increases and so does the frustration of those who think they should move up but are not selected for whatever reasons. This is also, where most people look for other options outside the company. Within this structure, the HR people are responsible for giving career advice. What a person can do or should do to enable her to continue growing with the organization.

Another stipulation of the career management model is that only identified individuals, earmarked for potential growth earlier in their career, can move forward. A lot of care is taken by the HR department at the recruitment and selection stage to pick those individuals who can really soar. In the first two years, the new recruits are tested in various roles and given various projects. Their performance is closely monitored and at the end of the two years, a decision is made regarding the ultimate potential of each of them. It is at that stage that their career paths are defined and laid out generally covering their entire stay but more specifically focused on the next 3-5 years. The brightest of them are put in a program called Road To Success (RTS), which enables them to cover the journey to the top in almost one third of the time it would take an average performer.

Most people have a problem with this decision regarding who is eligible for growth and who is not. People frequently question, albeit never openly, what gives HR the right to choose a person to become an RTS employee. Their point is that once you are picked, nothing anyone else may do would make him eligible for RTS. Quite rightly then, the HR keeps its CTS strictly confidential.

Another issue people have with the same system is the HR's choice of 'blockers'. Just as HR identifies people for RTS, they also identify people who have become blockers or have the potential to become blockers. Blockers are defined as those people who have a certain skill/knowledge etc., which enables them to do a job really well but block the path of those behind them because they cannot personally move upwards. HR's policy towards such people is to counsel them to leave the job and find something else to do. HR only does that once it has found and trained a person to replace the blocker.

The OD Consultant had identified the reason why people became blockers as follows:

Either at the recruitment level, the recruiters were not clear of the ultimate potential of the person or he was hired solely for the said job. For instance, if some one was hired for the position of Industrial Relations manager keeping in view his abilities and grasp over local law pertaining to labor etc, no thought at that point in time was given to his growth within the organization. Alternatively, after being assigned in various roles this person found his niche in a certain role or since he was so good in this role, he was never considered for any other role.

In her analysis of why careers are stalled, the consultant had shown the following:

The question we could pose could be 'How do careers get stalled?' Only by answering this question can we come to an understanding of what to do about them. The systemic analysis of the current situation gives us this:

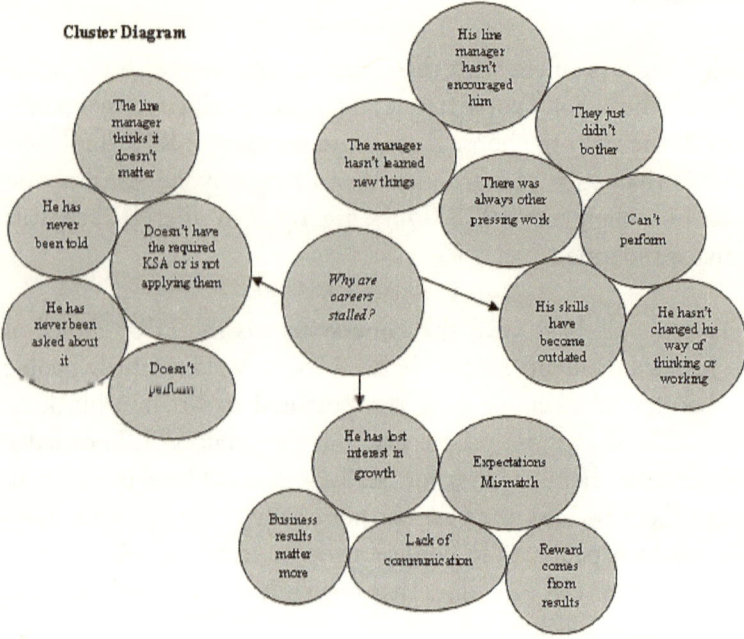

Looking closely at this diagram, we could discern the following underlying themes:

- Performance is directly proportional to interest,
- To grow, managers need new levels of knowledge, skills, and attitudes and they have to be made conscious of it,

- Lack of communication is a big cause of stalled careers,
- Such training needs to be imparted which is closely linked to performance (& eventual results) and line managers need to take responsibility for clarifying their expectations vis-à-vis organizational performance appraisal system,
- People whose careers get stalled are people whose managers never took an interest in their careers, and
- What is rewarded is done; focus is on results because that is what is rewarded.

On further analysis, the following reason becomes clear in terms of why careers are stalled:

| Managers don't take interest in developing their subordinates |

BECAUSE

| Everyone is focused on generating individual results |

BECAUSE

| This is what the Performance & Reward Management System recognizes |

The consultant then gave the problem statement as **'how to change the reward system to enable managers to start taking interest in the development of their subordinates' careers?'** Therefore, in her view, if the performance system was changed, people's careers will not be stalled and the organization would be rid of this plague of blockers.

PEOPLE & CULTURE

"Two things are bad for the heart-running uphill and running down people."
Bernard Gimbel

Pro Inc. had been lucky to attract a bright bunch of people over the past years. Apart from the fact that they had had a problem of retaining these young guns, the overall quality of people had been exemplary. This was mostly attributed to a good working environment and a competitive salary package. People were given a good exposure to the corporate world and quite a lot of training events either in house or outsourced were arranged.
[Ref.: This Thing Called Culture.]

The environment encouraged competition and everyone was always trying to prove to his or her superiors that he or she is worthy of the next coveted slot. The system of PA/DR also recognized this and hence everyone was caught in that spiral of individual performance. Given this scenario, every line manager balanced her hopes of moving up by using the subordinates' shoulders.

In an effort to cut costs and to make matters worse, the company had adopted a policy of hiring people on contract basis. What this meant in terms of costs was less pressure on the payroll. The contractual staff did not get any bonuses, or any other benefits but just a salary, which was good for some and not so good for others. What this meant in terms of morale was a sort of alienation. The contractual staff felt and in some people's perception were meant to feel their *'lightness of being.'* In other words, they felt inferior to the permanent staff. They were not required in many departmental meetings and did not have a feeling of being in on things. These were also the people whose shoulders were burdened with the weight of their line managers' promotions. Roughly, at least 20% of the company's employees were on contract and rumors were that this percentage was going to increase.

The managers on the other hand were not helping matters. Their attitude towards their staff was more like one might have towards the flies. Their eyes were focused on their own growth and while they did pay some attention to the development of their junior managers, they did not even bother with the problems and needs of the contractual staff. This sort of behavior had given birth to groupings. The managers or the *'suits'* had their own little elite group. The contract staff had their own group where they could get together and curse the managers of their choice. Then there were subgroups within the ranks of managers divided functionally, seniority wise, and according to pay scales. Obviously as in any organization, there were exceptions, but generally, the differences were accepted and respected as and where they stood.

Being a progressive organization, Pro Inc., regularly had a third party conduct a company wide Internal Employee Satisfaction Survey (IESS). The last year's survey results showed modest improvements in some areas and had highlighted certain areas for improvements as well. The summary results are as follows:

The objectives of the research were to identify how people perceive the application of what the management preaches. This included commitment to the vision, commitment to the people, the work environment and commitment to the espoused values of the company.

The results highlighted that 60% of the people felt that the espoused values of the company, which included:

Fostering empowered employees, fostering open mindedness, appreciating an enterprising spirit in people and appreciating and rewarding talent at all levels were just words on the wall. It was cited that the company did not offer personal fulfillment of individuals and there was very little opportunity provided to use ones own initiative.

The results also highlighted that 70% of the people felt that the culture was not as open as it was made out to be. 86% believed that there was no reward and recognition for team working. 78% believed that the line managers were not ready to listen (understand) the subordinates' point of views, forcing their own decisions instead of collaborating with their people. 67% pointed out an element of fear hindering open and honest communications especially at the grade 27-30 level of management.

While 89% of the people said that they thought the company's policies towards people development were at par with other comparable companies, a staggering 91% felt that there was an environment of mistrust in the company, which eventually led to a lot of bureaucracy. The most common bottleneck identified (76%) in the growth of individual careers was line manager's attitude and lack of planning. To the question of company's major problem, 84% people pointed out the loss of talented people. In addition, the most common reason cited for this problem was identified as top management's attitude.

On the brighter side, 82% of the people believed that the company was moving in the right direction of achieving its vision and possessed good planning skills. 72% believed that the people in the company had a strong drive to achieving its vision. 91% believed that the company's products were a result of consumer focus. 81% believed that the company had set high standards for everyone. 87% of the respondents showed high levels of confidence in company's ability to achieve its goals and objectives.

The survey results also showed that 90% of the people felt that our strength lies in culture which if improved would guarantee success. 86% people believed that improvement in teamwork could double the company's productivity. 81% pointed out that if leadership improved and became more people focused the current performance would be doubled. 81% people highlighted improvement in communication as one of the most critical aspects contributing to organization's growth.

Interestingly, one of the previous consultants who was hired by the HR department had also done some searching on the cultural aspects of the company as well. Her views were buried deep and forgotten, but here are some notes from her diary. These notes were taken from conducting several interviews with various people at various levels of the company, and silent observation:

Pro Inc. has people at every level with condescending attitudes downwards and kissing ass attitudes upwards. The only criteria for respect seem to be seniority and grade. Contractual employees and supervisory staff are looked down upon *(or at least that is their perception)* though no one admits it is so. People generally believe that if they can make their line managers happy and have good relationship with them, there are good chances for their growth. There have been many examples of company's star performers leaving for even lower paid jobs because they could not survive here on mere performance and they could not kiss ass. Senior managers demand/command that people suck up to them. It is like an unwritten norm. A good example in collective memory is of a bright young professional manager who could not retain his job simply because when the director walked in the room he remained seated while everyone else had risen up in respect!

This plague of protocol transcends all levels. As junior managers become senior, something automatically changes their attitudes. Interestingly enough, this protocol has to be judged and understood by the junior staff. For example, the senior managers would deny getting preferential treatment say when they go to a hotel. However, their junior staff know that they want it. Hence, they have to labor hard to get a VP a presidential suite in a hotel for example but on papers show that the hotel gave it to the company on a complimentary basis. In this way the senior manager would enjoy the luxuries that other members of the team will not be able to, yet claim that he did not cost the company extra.

Another cultural aspect is that of giving and getting credit. If the junior managers or supervisory staff do something well, like a project or an assignment, the line manager takes the credit and if the project fails or is delayed etc., then the person responsible for the execution 'gets it'. While people do not really think it is a big thing, they do feel and show this frustration that it is an unfair practice, and shows the inefficiency of the line managers.

Someone, who had decided to resign, shared a very enlightening experience. In his words, this was the most difficult decision he had ever had to make. It was difficult because he knew that he would not find the package he was getting here. Yet, he was willing to take his chances. In his view the package, this company gave, and the comfortable environment it provided was all very lucrative and one could really get used to it. When that happened, one would become complacent. When one would become complacent, one would tend to ignore many things, which he might not agree with and would tend to compromise on his values. It may be easy to leave early in one's career but as time passed on one would tend to play for keeps. In his view, those managers who were playing for keeps would never like to develop and groom others to take their place because they would know that they may not move too far ahead. It also encourages a risk-averse mindset. Hence, if HR department cannot counter this problem, this company would keep on losing talented people.

Having decided that the pay this company offers would take care of many of their individual problems, people tend to stick around and bear whatever comes with it. Hence, to keep their jobs, an unwritten practice is to not question and or challenge the higher authority. Although the written practice is to be able to challenge and question the line managers, which theoretically would show the capability of the person in question. No one does it because people who have done it have paid the price of being rooted out of the company. This also reflects the culture of the society the people are operating under, the underlying philosophy being 'not to rock the boat'. For majority of the people job security is of prime importance. Given the macro economic conditions of the country, people reluctantly go on until they drop, and, in this process, becoming entirely dependent upon the company to look out for them.

The most terrifying of all practices is that people are verbally asked and encouraged to talk openly and share their thoughts and feelings, give feedback etc. The company claims to have an open door policy as well. However, in reality, the feeling around various levels is that these are all tools for manipulation. The same is felt about the 360° feedback mechanism. Everyone feels at some level that the rule of this jungle is 'might is right' so might as well shut up and survive.

Another interesting aspect of the culture here has to do with the involvement of department head or even director in the petty day-to-day issues and simple grammatical mistakes in reports. The old man himself spares no time in humiliating even other VPs regardless of who else is present at the scene. Likewise, the other senior managers behave in the same fashion with their juniors, belittling and berating them at any opportune moment. People on the receiving end of this affectionate behavior complain that this behavior is exhibited even for small mistakes such as a spelling or grammatical errors. "Is this professionalism?" they cry out. They say that 'we are all trained in our specific fields so why are we treated as if we do not know anything?'

Another point for dissatisfaction amongst the employees is the abuse of the word teamwork. It is commonly known that in this company individual efforts are rewarded. However, ultra smart managers usually talked about teamwork as the thing to do and if someone was not doing their bidding, she could very easily be pointed out as not a team player. However, people did understand that teamwork is a cover for managers to use the people to get the projects accomplished successfully and move up the ladder. The general belief is that in the name of teamwork managers are making false commitments and are trying to manipulate their way to the top. Everyone stays quite because they do not have other options.

Another issue here at PI (Pro Inc.) is that of selecting the top performers from the very start. The VPs pinpoint some fortunate managers who are given the maximum exposure through training opportunities and special projects, which are deemed very valuable and important for the company. It is argued that these people are the most suitable candidates for fast growth. Undoubtedly, these are very bright individuals, but it can be argued that these are not the only ones. Hence, the question arises why only these few individuals are tried out, repeatedly. One case of a young management trainee stands out, about which even the top management does not question. This young man was singled out by the VPHR and grew to become the head of this department in a very short span of seven years. Obviously, people could very easily guess who the next VPHR will be.

Within this environment, it is easy for other bright individuals to be disheartened and fulfill their ambitions elsewhere. Hence, the belief that if you are not the 'chosen one', you could not compete for the top regardless of how hard you tried. At the end of the day, when it came to survival, many people just buried themselves in their work.

However, there are pros and cons of this kind of behavior as well. The good thing about it is that the level of productivity increases and the bad thing is that it only lasts for a very short period. In the end, this person would either leave to retain his /her sanity or become a company vegetable. In either case, it would mean a loss to the overall organization. What would be and probably is more disastrous in this situation is that the managers/leaders at the top would not even realize what effects their decisions are having, and would probably fail to acknowledge the loss due to them. They would likely say that it is all about individual choice. Many people referred to this phenomenon in the following way: "It's like getting screwed while your hands are tied at the back, and you are expected to smile and say everything is alright and thank you very much!" this is how some people described how it is like working here.

I wonder why people would choose to continue working here. The answer given to me is that there are not any comparably good jobs available, and the HR department knows that very well.

Another aspect of this culture is late sittings. While everyone cribs about it, almost everyone does it. It is perceived that if you are sitting late you are showing your dedication and commitment. Those who do not practice this are questioned in terms of their loyalty to their work group. While the top management consistently sends out this message, at least verbally, that we care about your family life and the time you need to spend at home, in reality the kind of tasks and the kind of deadlines given to the people compel them to sit way beyond normal working hours. The dilemma is that not a whole lot of work is being accomplished this way, but people seem to have realized that it is the best way to make a good impression on their respective bosses.

Those people who do their work on time and are excellent performers would be targeted for 'humorous criticism' from their bosses. The focus would be on the time spent working in the office and not the actual results and products delivered. In fact, more emphasis is given on coming on time as opposed to delivering to the plan.

Another thing, which I find weird here, is that although people are sent to various training program some of them being quite expensive, everyone keeps his or her cell phone on so that they can constantly stay in touch with the office. If on the request of the trainer they have to switch off their cell phones, their line managers would reprimand them. On the other hand, people look forward to this excursion of going out for a training session because it takes them away from the office. In other words, training means an outing. While the company does expend on training and development activities, no bottom line link is ever established.

The way I see it, it is a give and take situation. The company tries to squeeze the most out of the people working for it. Conversely, the people give only that much output which is necessary, and try to squeeze as much out of the company as possible. The operative principle seems to be *'the company is going to use you till it needs you, so use it till you need it.'*

THE FINAL QUESTION

"We can't dig a hole in a new place by digging the same hole deeper."
Edward De Bono

If you were given the charge of making this company come out on the top, what would you do? Would you change the nature of the business? Would you give in to the pressures? Would you do nothing and let things be? Would you try to change the culture of this organization and if so, where would you start? Would you try to redesign the organization and if so, how would you design it?

These are the kind of questions that a manager/leader has to face all the time, more so in the example that I have tried to build over the previous pages. Real life is like this, it happens when you are making other plans as someone once said. Hence, the ultimate question once again: WHAT DO WE DO?

"It was the best of times, it was the worst of times, it was the age of wisdom, it was the age of foolishness, it was the epoch of belief, it was the epoch of incredulity, it was the season of light, it was the season of darkness, it was the spring of hope, it was the winter of despair, we had everything before us, we had noting before us . . ."

Charles Dickens, A Tale of Two Cities

EPILOGUE

Perhaps you do have more questions now than you had before you started reading this. As I said before, that is all right because now we need to figure out how to get things right. It is about the choices we make that determine the direction our lives take. So is the case with any organization such as PI. Perhaps you have experienced some thing like this, may be you are going through it right now. Whatever the case may be, it is up to you, up to us, to ensure that we have answers to the situation described previously. Let us explore!!!

ORGANIZATION AS A GARDEN

Many years ago, in an interview, I was asked what I thought was the role played by HR in any organization. I said then, as I still believe today, that HR manager or the HR department plays the role of a 'Gardener', and that from this perspective the organization is like a garden. The gardener or as we call him the *"mali"* has the job of nurturing the garden as a whole by taking care of each and every plant in that garden including the grass. His responsibility lies in making sure that healthy leaves and branches grow, weak ones' growth is helped and facilitated, and dead wood is removed. At that time I hadn't read the book by James Collins, **Built To Last**, in which he and his team describe one of the characteristics of a visionary company under the heading of 'try a lot of stuff and keep what works' in the following manner:

"The evolutionary process is like 'branching and pruning.' If you add enough branches to a tree (variation) and intelligently prune the deadwood (selection), then you'll likely evolve into a collection of healthy branches well positioned to prosper in an ever changing environment."

Hence HR plays that vital role of nurturing this garden. When and how much fertilizer to give to the whole garden *(Training & Development)*; when and how much to water *(Job Enrichment)*; which plant to be placed where *(Selection & Placement)*; which plant to remove, prune/cut its dead branches *(Job Rotation)*; cleaning the fallen tree twigs, leafs *(Succession Planning)* etc., and so on so forth. All of this and more in an effort to develop and beautify the garden, making it look neat, clean, and healthy. All of this is done in line with the envisioned future of the garden, or in other words, how the garden would or should look in a couple of years or less.

HR'S ROLE AS A GARDENER

It all starts with the vision of the organization. The HR people must ask these questions and take action based on the answers to these questions: what will the organization look like in the years to come (5, 10, or 15 years)? What will it take to make it look like what we've envisioned? Where do we start and what is the first thing that we need to do today that will ensure that we achieve our long term vision as well as our short term goals? And finally, what would be the second, third and fourth steps and so forth?

HR people, in my view, have a responsibility similar to that of a gardener, in terms of producing a garden (read organization). However, our work is slightly more taxing because we are dealing with 'live', 'flesh & blood' human beings and not just some dumb plants. We deal with more intangibles, we operate in a highly dynamic and rapidly evolving environment where there are no clearly defined boundaries between 'changing seasons', and more often than naught, we operate in totally unpredictable circumstances. Here, in this garden, we don't often know what action will produce what effect.

It is claimed that if you talk to your plants, show them love and affection, besides all the other things that you have to do, they grow rather healthier than those plants that don't get talked to. I believe there is some research to prove that. If you find this weird, try managing a multitude of people from different walks of life and from varied socio-economic dispositions and using all the HR tricks in the bag to develop and nurture them, and above all, showing them love and affection. Phew! I truly sympathize with everyone in HR.

ORGANIZATION DEFINED

We tend to use this word 'organization' rather casually. I believe that if we dig a little deeper into its meaning and its implications, we'll find more meaning in our work as HR professionals.

The Concise Oxford Dictionary 8th Edition, 1990, defines the word **organization** as follows: the act or instance of organizing; the state of being organized: an organized body can be anything like a business, government department or a charity etc. This word (organization) stems from the word **organize** which is defined as: to give an orderly structure, to systematize, make arrangements, form into an organic whole: make into a living being or tissue. This word (organize) stems from the word **organism** which means: a living individual consisting of a single cell or a group of inter-dependent parts sharing the life processes, a whole with interdependent parts compared to a living being. *(In the process I also looked up words such as organic, organza and orgasm but they don't have any relevance here.)*

My interpretation is thus, an organization is a coming together of various 'parts' to form a 'whole' in order to achieve something that individually these parts couldn't possibly achieve. Hence it is a dynamic process rather than a static one; it is based upon unifying and compelling goal(s) or target(s) or a vision to attract the parts to come together. And we, the HR professional or practitioners have the job or an obligation to nurture, develop, and manage this ever changing and evolving process of coming together to achieve our collective goals.

WHAT HR CONTRIBUTES

Corporately speaking, how effectively work is organized to achieve the stated goals efficiently, whatever they might be, is then the HR professionals' primary responsibility. At least that's what I believe our role has to be in the new millennium. This 'organization' of minds, bodies and souls to work in a certain direction, towards a sought after goal requires a lot more than interviewing skills or understanding of labor laws etc. We know that once this collage of individuals forms an organization, it is no longer a hodgepodge of different individuals but a living, breathing entity in its own right, with its own life cycle, and peculiar behaviors. As HR practitioners we are dealing with not individual identities but a collective identity we usually refer to as the organization. And just like every other thing alive, if not taken care, it can very easily rot and perish.

If the organization fails to achieve its stated objectives, then one of the reasons for its failure or inadequacy would be the inability of its HR department to enable it to do so. Primarily, it would be HR, which would have to take the leading role in reviving and sustaining an organization's success in its field of endeavor. In fact, CIPD, one of the leading HR professionals' bodies in UK requires its students to be certified marketers before they can be recognized as HR professionals! Is it any wonder?

MINDSET

Traditionally the mindset about the people in HR or of the HR people themselves has been far removed from the business's performance. Just like accountants, who are unsympathetically referred to as 'bean counters', HR practitioners have been looked upon as record keepers; a job which could be anything but value adding. Keeping files of or on people, counting how many leaves they are left with, arguing who is eligible for what benefit, labor negotiations and so forth. Undoubtedly all these things have to be dealt with and also undoubtedly HR department is the best place for this to be dealt with. My concern is the mindset.

If we believe that HR is the gardener of the organization, if we accept that this organizing is an evolving and dynamic process of various elements coming together to achieve some goal, and if we understand that we achieve that goal through work, then if the goal is not being achieved we have to change the way we work, the way we organize. If we accept all of this as our primary responsibility, then we are aligned with the business and its vision, then we have the right mindset. And in this mindset the record keeping role takes a back seat. In this mindset the role of HR as the guardian of status quo changes to become the torchbearer of change. In other words, we just can't afford to be rigid and outdated, and if we are, we are not practicing HR even if we call ourselves HR people.

If we have organized to put a PC on every table in every household, and somehow we aren't able to do that we have plenty of modern tools and techniques to enable ourselves to do that. We could restructure, re-engineer, train our people in new skills, enrich jobs, devise a better performance & reward management system et cetera, et cetera. The point is that we have organized to do something, and if we aren't doing it right we need to re-organize in the best possible way to achieve our objectives. And this process must continue till we achieve that what we were looking for to begin with.

THE HR DILEMMA OF THIS MILLENNIUM

And here lies the dilemma. In today's world where everyone is going for stretch goals, where the marketplace changes faster than the blink of an eye, and the goals have to change accordingly and this seems to be a relentless loop, with no signs of slowing down ever, what are HR people supposed to do? Should we change our organizations every year? Should we change our structures every time there is a shift in the market? Should we just put our people in a never ending spiral of organizing and reorganizing and so on? Should we change their job profiles every year? What happens once we find what we are looking for? I mean, where does it all end?

I think our answers lie in the future. But we must look at the past to begin with. In times of less upheaval and more predictability, bureaucratic structures of management sufficed. Every man for a job, even if it was a monotonous one. The principles of scientific management thrived. Then the market changed, competition emerged, giants crumbled. The information age arrived sooner than everyone's expectations. And who knows where it's going to take us all. In a highly regarded Fortune magazine article written by executive editor Walter Kiechel III entitled, **'How we will work in the year 2000'**, six trends were identified, which I think shed light on the work's future:

- *The average company will become smaller, employing fewer people,*
- *The traditional hierarchical organization will give way to a variety of organizational forms, the network of specialists foremost amongst these,*
- *Technicians ranging from computer repairmen to radiation therapists will replace manufacturing operatives as the worker elite,*

- *The vertical division of labor will be replaced by a horizontal division,*
- *The paradigm of doing business will shift from making a product to providing a service, and*
- *Work itself will be redefined as constant learning with more high-order thinking and less nine-to-five clock punching.*

Although this article was for the West, I see it happening here in Pakistan. We have all heard about and most probably experienced the massive downsizing exercises. We have all heard about or experienced flat organizations, shop floor workers are being replaced by more technically advanced and educated workforce, and newer terms like 'knowledge management' and 'learning organization' are being heard in corporate corridors. IT is becoming a major force in all organizations. Everyone is talking about change management. Flexible working hours are being practiced in some organizations here as well. The concept of work, as one might visualize sitting in front of the computer in an office, has changed to having a laptop sitting on your lap on a flight from Karachi to Islamabad, and so forth. However, surprisingly, many organizations even now are doing all of this and still within the hierarchies their forefathers left for them. Isn't it any wonder then that these organizations are not tapping into their own potentials?

Looking at what the future has in store for us, we the HR practitioners must act proactively. Looking at what's in store for us, what is the best way to organize our work (the organization)? I think the answer lies in what we expect the Pakistani market will be like in the years to come. This demands of us a comprehensive understanding and knowledge of the market dynamics. In essence then, we have to be at least at par with our marketing counterparts, finance people, production people and legal affairs people, in addition to the HR peer group. One way to do this would be to conduct a SWOT analysis of the PEST factors. Having done that we would be in a better position to ascertain the role HR needs to play.

FINAL THOUGHTS

Once we have generated this knowledge, we can then sit down and come up with a way to organize and design our organization. We can then talk about what sort of policies we need to enable our organizations to really deliver. We can then talk about our performance standards and ways to measure them, our structures, and our systems, everything customized to our specific business needs, environments and goals.

What we do as HR professionals is full of impact. If you agree with what I have said here, then you must also agree that our responsibility to our respective organizations is more than any of our counterparts. However, our role is of 'king makers' or 'directors' rather than 'kings' or 'actors'. We work behind the scenes but if we and only if we do our work right can the people working on the screen can get their act together. It is, nevertheless, a combined effort, where most of the time people like us will not get the credit when things go right, and always get the blame when they don't. But hey, it is a living!

THE ROLE OF TRAINING & DEVELOPMENT

In the army, training is given to soldiers before they enter the battlefield. In organizations, people are given training while they are in the battle! There is a place in California where the US army practices the art of war in replicated or envisioned war scenarios, with live ammunition! This ensures that when real war comes, they are ready.

Most of us in times of peace or war work for some organization, which is fighting in some market place. However, most organizations do not have a kind of a training laboratory where we could practice what we would do in the real market place with changing scenarios. One could argue that all the business schools of the world are just that, training labs for people like us who want to make our careers in one field of the business or another.

I for one agree with Henry Mintzberg's point of view made three decades ago: *"Management schools will begin the serious training of managers when skill training takes its place next to cognitive learning. Cognitive learning is detached and informational, like reading a book or listening to a lecture. No doubt, much important cognitive material must be assimilated by the manager-to-be. But cognitive learning no more makes a manager than it makes a swimmer. The latter will drown the first time he jumps into the water if his coach never takes him out of the lecture hall, gets him wet, and gives him feedback on his performance. Our management schools need to identify the skills managers use, select students who show potential in these skills, put the students into situations where these skills can be practiced and give them systematic feedback on their performance."*[4]

Many other have made similar observations. The message is simple: from all perspectives, competence in personal, interpersonal, and group skills is a critical pre-requisite for success in management. Strong analytical and quantitative skills are important, but they are not sufficient. In a survey of 110 Fortune 500 CEOs:

- 87 percent were satisfied with the level of competence and analytical skills of business school graduates
- 68 percent were satisfied with conceptual skills of graduates
- Only 43 percent of the CEOs were satisfied with graduates' management skills
- Only 28 percent were satisfied with their interpersonal skills

A study conducted in America investigated factors that best accounted for financial success of forty major manufacturing companies over a period of five years (Hanson, 1986). The question was, "What explains the financial success of the firms that are highly effective?" The five most powerful predictors were identified and assessed:

Market Share *(assuming that the higher the market share of a firm, the higher its profitability)*

Firm Capital Intensity *(assuming that more a firm is automated and up-to-date in technology and equipment, the more profitable it is.)*

Size of the firm in Assets *(assuming that economies of scale and efficiencies can be used in large firms to increase profitability)*

Industry Average Return on Sales *(assuming that firms would reflect the performance of a highly profitable industry)*

The ability of managers to effectively manage their people *(assuming that an emphasis on good people management helps produce profitability in firms.)*

Surprisingly the statistical analysis revealed that the last factor *(ability of managers to manage effectively)* was three times more powerful than all other factors combined in accounting for firms' financial success over a five-year period. Good management was more important than all other factors in predicting profitability!

A study conducted by the US Office of the Controller of the Currency, was an investigation in determining the reasons of failure of national banks in the 1980s. *(162 banks had failed in that period.)* Two major factors were found to account for the record number of bank failures in that eight-year period: distressed economic conditions and poor management. However, the relative impact of these two factors was somewhat surprising. 89 percent of the failed banks were judged to have had poor management. Only 35 percent of the failed banks had experienced depressed economic conditions in the region in which they operated, and in only 7 percent of the cases was the depressed economic condition the sole cause of bank failure! The government research team concluded the following:

"We found oversight and management deficiencies to be the primary factors that resulted in bank failure, in fact poor policies, planning, and management were significant causes of failure in 89% of the banks surveyed. The quality of a bank's board and management depends on the experience, capability, judgment, and integrity of its directors and senior officers. Banks that had directors and managers with significant shortcomings made up a large portion of the banks that we surveyed."

In another study, an effort was made to identify what constitutes effective management. For this study, a sample of managers was used who were rated as highly effective managers in their own organizations. The industries covered in this sample included business, healthcare education, and state government. The questions asked to these successful managers in various interviews included:

- How have you become so successful in this organization?
- Who fails and who succeeds in this organization and why?
- If you had to train someone to take your place, what knowledge and skills would you make certain that person possessed.
- If you could design an ideal course or training program to teach you to be better manager, what would it contain?
- Think of other effective managers you know. What skills do they demonstrate that explain their success?

The analysis produced 60 characteristics of effective managers. The top ten skills identified were as follows:

i. *Verbal communication (including listening)*
ii. *Managing time & stress*
iii. *Managing individual decisions*
iv. *Recognizing, defining, and solving problems*
v. *Motivating & influencing others*
vi. *Delegating*
vii. *Setting goals & articulating a vision*
viii. *Self-awareness*
ix. *Team building*
x. *Managing conflict*

Three notable characteristics are typical of these skills; first, the skills are behavioral, which means that anyone can learn and improve upon them. Second, they are paradoxical. They are neither all soft and humanistic in orientation, nor all hard driving and directive. Hence, what is required is a mastery of diverse and seemingly contradictory skills. Finally, these critical skills are interrelated and overlapping. No effective manager performed one skills or one set of skills independent of others.

In most of my training programs, I emphasize the **KSA** model. K stands for knowledge, which will get you in an organization at a certain level. S stands for skills, which will help you move up in the organization. And A stands for attitude, which will determine how far up you can go! Similarly, at operational levels technical skills are important. As one moves up, I believe, that managerial skills take precedence, and managerial skills are about managing people and their behaviors.

Evidence suggests that management skills training can have significant impact on the bottom line performance of a firm.

The US Postal Service did a study in which, 49 of their largest 100 post offices in America were evaluated. An important question in the study was, "How can we make post offices more effective?" Productivity and service quality both were monitored over a 5-year period. The two major factors that had impact on these effectiveness measures were: 1) the degree of mechanization *(automation)*, and 2) investment in training. Two kinds of trainings were provided: 1) maintenance training *(training in maintaining and operating the equipment)* and 2) management training *(training in developing management skills)*. The overall conclusion of the study was, *"Performance levels in these organizations vary systematically and predictably as training levels vary. The training-performance relationship is positive and statistically significant."* More specifically, the study found the following:

That providing management training was more important than providing maintenance training in accounting for improved productivity and service in the post offices.

Both kinds of training were more important than having automated and up-to-date equipment in the post offices.

Low-tech offices out performed high-tech offices when managers were provided with managerial training. In short, its 5-year study convinced the US Postal Service that helping employees to develop managerial skills was the best way to improve organizational effectiveness.

In too many companies training and development is considered as a 'nice to do' activity, which may be done when the going is easy and budgets are plenty. Come the hard times, training budgets are the first to be cut. When the going gets tough, the focus is on just getting the work done and meeting the targets. There is a saying, *'If you always do what you've always done, you'll always get what you've always got.'* If the preceding examples show anything, it is the need of training and development for and during the hard times. The problem is, once again, the mind set. Do you consider training to be a pleasure activity, rating it in terms of how much fun it was? The answer to this question is the key. If it is a break from the monotony of the daily routine, which it also is nevertheless, then it is of no real value. However, if you and your line managers genuinely believe that it is essential to your success at your job, then it is a whole new ball game altogether.

HUMAN RESOURCE PLANNING

To ensure that an organization's performance stays on course, and its needs consistently met, requires talented and motivated people, who can get the work done efficiently and effectively. This requires some visionary thinking in terms of career planning, performance management, employee development, and succession. Who else but the HR department can take on this responsibility? After all they are the so called 'king makers.'

HRP is the process through which organizations are managed. It must start with a philosophy towards people management and development, which must strike a balance with organizational needs. Hence, the first step to HRP has to look at and into the vision and objectives of the organization as a whole and its link with people performance.

HRP must also be able to address the career progression of people from the point of hiring to the point of departure at any given stage due to any reason like death, retirement, resignation etc. This presupposes that certain questions have been answered. Questions like:

- Have the career paths for every given position in any given department been defined?
- Are the promotion criteria established and communicated?
- Is everyone aware of the time durations and age limits defining the growth of any individual within the organization, so that he may ascertain how far he can go and in how much time?
- Are their enough people with potential in the funnel to replace those who leave? Etc.

ORGANIZATIONAL PERFORMANCE & PEOPLE MOTIVATION

Balancing the growth of the organization with the growth of its people then is the real challenge for HR. So where does one start? In my view it must start far ahead in the future, say 30 years from today. The visionary HR leader would ask what would be the shape of things to come in this time, given the realities of today and the dreams of tomorrow. This futurist approach would help the HR leader to define the shape of the organization. Hence, certain questions would require a great deal of pondering keeping in view the market dynamics.

One must be able to foresee what this organization will look like in the future: is it flatter? Have the hierarchies gone? How is it structured? What kind of environmental pressures are affecting the business? What technological advances the company has made or is using or what technologies are available for use. What functions have been outsourced? What functions have been added? What does the organization want to achieve? Other considerations may be as follows: how are people being evaluated? What jobs are they being called upon to do? How is their work structured? What is the ratio of managers to workers, males to females? What is the average age a person is being hired at? What is the average length of stay at the company? At what age is he leaving the company? How happy are the pensioners? Etc, etc, etc.

Then one must focus on the knowledge, skills and attitudes of the people who are or will be working in such an organization. What is the knowledge level of the new entrants? What is the required knowledge base? How quickly do they develop skills to help them achieve their goals? What is the success rate of the projects they undertake? What is the morale level required to work in the company's current environment? What sort of politics might or have emerged due to the changes? What skills are required for success, growth, promotions? How far does one go with a certain level of knowledge, skills, and attitude? What sources are available for their development? How is this linked with their performance? What is the rate of growth within the organization? What opportunities are available and what are made available for people to rise vertically and horizontally? And so forth.

At the heart of HRP then, lies the issue of balancing people motivation/needs and organizational performance/needs. The problem could be stated *as "How to balance people motivation with organizational performance?"*

The first consideration in this regard must be to identify the motivators and de-motivators. A partial list may include the following:

Factors of Motivation & De-motivation	
Motivation	*De-motivation*
Money	Lack of involvement
Benefits	Working hours (long)
Challenging work	Static job
Exposure	Long stay at any single job
Training	Routine work
Perception of being valued	No prospects for growth
Promotion	Lack of communication
Growth opportunities	Perception of unfair/inferior treatment
Higher increments	Nepotism
Bonuses	Mismatch of expectations

The second step would be to list the factors affecting organizational performance. These may include things like:

- Market performance
- Internal environment/culture
- Business growth/development
- Costs
- Target achievement

- Morale of people
- Etc.

HRP must take into account all these factors when planning for the future. This can be done with the help of a technique known as scenario planning.

Let us say that an organization sees its future in the following way: due to increasingly strict regulations and higher taxes, the cost of manufacturing has increased. To cope with this increase, the company has relied heavily on technologically advanced machinery and has invested a lot in it. However, due to this investment, the reliance on labor, which was once cheap and readily available, has also declined steeply. However, with this technological increase, the need for highly skilled, intelligent, and educated workers has also increased. On the other hand, in the market the product demand is decreasing and is expected to continue sliding.

Therefore, the company has scaled down its operations considerably. Production has been outsourced in such a way that all its various production plants have been made independent companies, which means that they can sell to the original parent company as well as other interested buyers. However, the company retains control over its brands, brand quality, and image. The labor is highly skilled though few in numbers. More and more reliance is placed on a huge network of suppliers, distributors, wholesalers, and retailers. All warehouses have been privatized as well.

The company has identified and defined three main processes fundamental to its survival and growth:

Getting the products to the Market: this has generated a new breed of managers called 'supply chain managers.' This group of managers includes selected people from the previous functions of production, procurement, finance, and marketing. This group is responsible for achieving sales, profitability, and cost targets of the company.

Getting the product to the consumers: this has generated another group of managers whose job is to advise, consult, and help the network to enhance their sales and profitability. These managers are called 'relationship managers.'

This group includes selected people from marketing and finance, serving as the front end and back end respectively.

Managing stakeholders: the managers in this group are called 'corporate brand & image managers.' Their job is to ensure smooth flow of business with respect to financial operations/institutions, excise, taxation, government agencies, investors, shareholders and so forth. Managers in this group are people from areas of legal department, public relations, finance, and marketing.

Finally, the company has also identified one critical sub-process, which helps the core processes from end to end:

Managing the backend processes: This has produced a group of managers who specialize in managing the people related and IT related issues and act as the business facilitators or enablers for the other three groups, enabling them to deliver results. People from HR and IT make up this lot. They are called the 'organization managers.'

Suppose that today this company is, as so many others like it, a traditional, hierarchical, pyramid sort of a company, with functional domains and fiefdoms and so forth. What does it need to do today to be able to become what it needs to become tomorrow? You would probably guess, a strategy of managing change, and that would be right. How can this company manage this transition and more pertinent to our discussion, what role can or should HR play in helping the organization attain its future so as the organization continues to perform while the people remain motivated to work here?

RECRUITMENT & SELECTION

The first step may be taken at the policy level regarding the recruitment and selection of future employees. The first question that must be answered is *'is the company interested in hiring generalists or specialists?'* This needs a definition of both terms. Here is one:

- A generalist is a manager who can work equally well in various disciplines such as marketing or finance or HR etc., and as such possesses general management skills such as coordination, planning, communication and so forth.
- A specialist is one who is extremely good in some specific aspect or discipline such as advertising *(in marketing)* or training & development *(in HR)* within a larger subject. In addition, he is not good in overall coordination and cannot perform with the same efficiency and effectiveness at some other post in the company.

If the first approach is used then the company would be looking to hire people from a broad category of fields, revolve them around in the company, develop their leadership skills in order to ensure a hefty supply of leadership at the top. This would also mean that all the specialized work would be outsourced. If the second approach were used, then the company would need to divide the growth/career paths for the specialists and generalists, giving/paying extra to the specialists while the generalists are groomed for the top.

In either case, clear communication regarding career progression is required. For generalists a possible period to reach the top, performance standards, and career development opportunities must be laid out so that there are no ambiguities. For specialists it would be a simple matter of contributing at a certain level, at certain performance level, and perhaps retiring with hefty benefits.

Supposing a company uses both kinds of people, and for the generalists, who could be called 'fast trackers', the company has laid out a full development plan. This may look something like this generic process map:

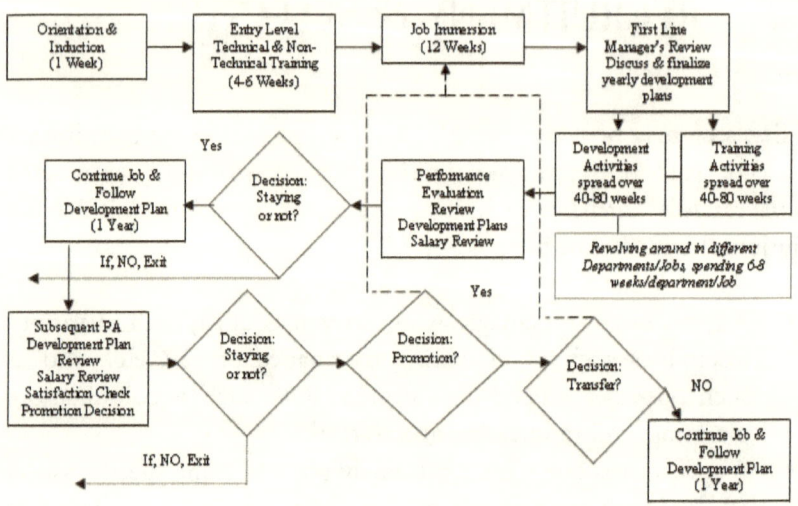

The story reads like this: a person is hired and goes through the initiation rights and is given an overview of the organization. The person is given or is put through essential training programs required. Then he or she is immersed in the job for which he/she was hired. After he or she has gotten some hands on experience, the line manager sits with him/her and develops the development plan for one year. After the stipulated period is over, the person's performance is reviewed and at this point in time it is discussed whether he or she would like to continue. If the answer is yes then this person goes on following the development plans and the job. If the answer is no, then over a period of one-three months, this person leaves while the organization looks for another. The second review period comes and same process is revised. This time around, some other decisions may also be considered. These include the question of whether this person should be promoted, i.e., has he/she fulfilled the promotion criteria. Secondly, should the manager consider keeping him/her in the same department/job or transfer to another department where he/she may perform better or where there is a need. If the person is to be promoted, then the process restarts at the job immersion level at the new job. If not he/she continues as before if he/she is doing well here. If he/she is not doing well some other functions, jobs, or departments may be considered.

CAREER MANAGEMENT

For an organization to manage careers of many individuals, it has to know the career options available in the organization. In a retail environment, for instance, a person can be hired at sales executive level, move up to department manager, become a store manager and move on to become retail operations director or VP. Alternatively, a person can start in sales, move up to become store merchandising manager, then the chief buyer and finally VP or director merchandising. Another option available to a person could be to start as sales executive, move up to marketing manager, then to regional marketing manager and finally VP or director marketing. Hence, many options are available depending upon the specific areas of strengths for any given individual. Graphically, it would look something like the following:

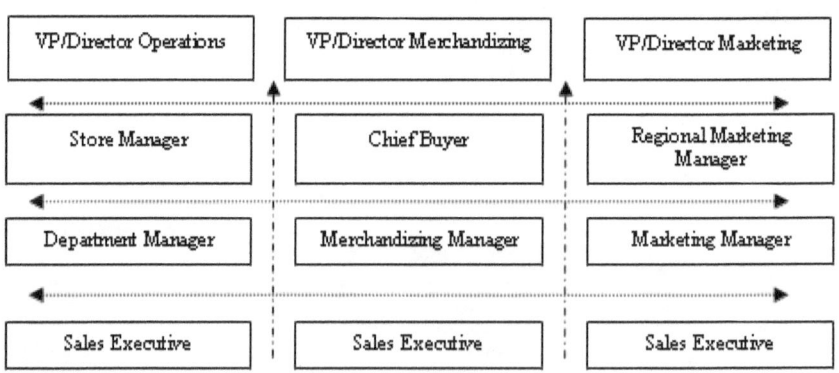

As it may be obvious, any person starting a career as sales executive has many career options. She can try for operations, merchandizing, or marketing specializations. Additionally, she has the luxury to get experience at different levels of various different roles. For ease of calculation, let us say that the period available to reach the top spot is 24 years. In this case, she can start as sales executive, in 3-6 years become the department manager. If she has a flare for marketing then she can move to become the marketing manager and perform for another 3-6 years. On proving her mettle, she becomes the regional manager and finally ends up as VP marketing. She can, if she prefers it that way, become a specialist early on. By starting in sales, moving into the merchandizing line and staying there. If she were a fast tracker, the organization would definitely want to groom her and would then like to get her through all the various facets of this organization plus some others not shown here like finance, legal affairs etc., and make her ready for the CEO position in 15-20 years.

For complex organizations, this may not be as simple. In organizations where there is an abundance of departments like production, procurement, marketing, finance, IT, HR, legal, public relations with many sub-departments each, the above-mentioned example would not be relevant. Keeping the levels to four, let us say that the following designations exist:

Career Table:

Marketing		Finance		Production		
Field Sales	Brands	Operations	Marketing	Production	Design	Maintenance
Head of Marketing		Corporate Finance Manager		Factory Manager		
National Sales Manager	Group Brand Manager	Operations Finance Manager	Marketing Finance Manager	Production Manager	Product Design Manager	Maintenance Engineer
Regional Manager	Brand Manager	Financial Services Manager	Planning Manager	Shift Manager	Quality Assurance Manager	Maintenance Service Manager
Area Manager	Brand Executive	Cost Accountant	Financial Analyst	Team Leader	Product Researcher	Shift Service Manager

Supposing in this organization, just like the previous example, the period available to anyone reaching the top position, which is the director level, is 24 years. It would be very difficult to spend an equal amount of time in each position and still perform at peak in terms of contributing to the growth of the organization. This would also require a very comprehensive educational background in engineering, finance, marketing and so forth. The jack-of-all-trades strategy would not work very well here. A person would have to be hired in any given department and groomed to grow within that line, say finance, with slight flirtations in other areas to get an overall view.

Another view towards managing people's careers could be to manage them via their grades. Suppose that the remunerations at each level are the same. This means that whether you are an area manager, brand executive, accountant, team leader, product researcher, or shift service manager, you get the same package. The grading system based on the seniority works like this: at area manager level, you are G1, at regional manager level you are at G2, and so forth. Finally, you have 24 years to go from G1 to G4, which means that on average you have to move up each level in maximum six years. In this scenario, if you were to ask, *"Where would I be in 10 years from now?"* a complete answer could be that *"you would be in G2 depending upon your performance and exactly which department or designation depends upon your interests."*

SUCCESSION PLANNING

The recruitment policy and strategies, training & development activities, and performance management system are and have to be closely linked with the succession planning for any company. Simply put the task here is to ensure that the right people are available at the right places. This is made possible by careful selection of potential leaders, meticulous development of talent and appropriate evaluation of their performances and potential.

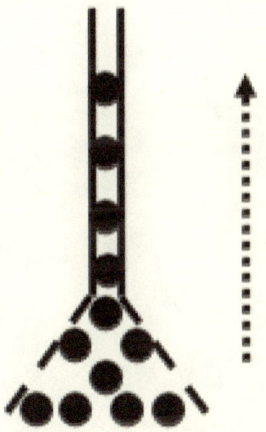

As opposed to popular beliefs about developing 'one' successor to any given post, my view is that all the time there should be many potential successors available. The dilemma is that we tend to follow a funnel approach to career growth. As one moves up the hierarchies the funnel gets smaller, letting fewer and fewer people to move up.

Another approach could be to assess personalities of the individuals along with other assessments, and place people according to the potential of their personalities. One such instrument the MBTI[5] helps do just that.

The concept of pre-requisites comes in very handy in providing a clear guideline as to who can succeed whom. For instance to be eligible for becoming a CEO there could be guidelines saying that a person needs to have gone through certain training programs, have had a certain amount of experience in various posts, designations and given a prescribed standard of output at each and every level.

PERFORMANCE MANAGEMENT

Performance management can be either evaluative in nature or developmental. If it is evaluative then it will be measuring past successes and failures and people's salaries would be based upon their past performances. If it were developmental in nature, it would focus more on how we could develop our people to take on the future challenges. As such, the first approach is past oriented and the second future oriented.

If the company is using an evaluative model, then, using the previous example a cost accountant's performance will be judged as per the tasks given to him in his role. How successfully has he done his job and what has been his rate of achievement. In the second model, his performance would be judged in terms of how close he has come to exhibiting the capabilities of the next position, which is that of financial services manager.

Both models may have their own pros and cons. However, both require a very clear understanding and communication of the job descriptions and success criteria at each level. Only when the expectations from the job are clear and benchmarks have been established, can performance be assessed. It would be a travesty if for instance, the criteria for success emphasize individual performances, and people are rated on their team efforts.

An example may clarify this further. Suppose we want to rate a sales person's performance working in a retail environment. The criteria we may use to rate his performance may include: number of customers he serves, sales per customer, increase in sales per customer, magnitude of each sale per customer and so forth. Therefore, if this person has been averaging $100/customer and making a sale of $1000/day, we can safely say that he serves 10 customers per day. If his average increases to $150/customer while the number of customers stays constant, we can say that he has improved his performance. If his average stays the same but the total sales he rings up increases to $1500/day, then his performance has not improved, only the number of customers walking in the store has increased. We could also monitor if this sales person is selling more 'small ticket items' or 'big ticket items.' This would be the difference between selling ten items worth $1 each as opposed to selling one item worth $10. In summary, exact quantitative and qualitative criteria need to be established, communicated, and then evaluated.

Performance then is a function of a job and various tasks within that job. In cases where no link has been established between a job and required performance, a job analysis needs to be done. That is only half of the story though. Performance is also a function of the training a person is given in order for him to do his job effectively.

JOB DESIGN

This must be done keeping in view two objectives: the organizational objectives must be achieved, and person doing the job must remain motivated. Whatever the job maybe, elements of performance and motivation must be built in. Therefore, each job should have certain characteristics like, it should be fulfilling and provide an enriching experience to the person doing it so that she enjoys doing it. The job should also have a clear link to some rewards, either monetary or non-monetary or both, to provide an extra incentive for the individual or team doing that job.

TRAINING & DEVELOPMENT

All T&D activities are a source of motivation regardless of what kind of training it may be. However, its real value lies in affecting change in someone's performance vis-à-vis his behavior, attitude, and skill level. The more accurate the performance appraisal, in terms of identifying the gaps in performance, the more accurately the trainings can be given to the individual.

In order to ascertain the gaps some quantitative as well as qualitative benchmarks are required. This process needs to be as objective as humanly possible. However, it is quite difficult. If a success criterion is the ability of a person to take initiative then how can one assess, albeit make a judgment, about whether a person does take initiative or not.

Given that some subjectivity will always be there in assessing someone's performance, the performance assessment process may be divided into assessing the individual's performance in terms of achieving his targets, and identifying the gaps which if fulfilled can improve his performance. As an example, we can say that a sales person objective was to achieve the given sales target of $X. let us also assume that he achieves 75% of the target. His increment would then reflect his performance. However, we want a 100% performance, so how would we bridge that gap of 25%? This would force the salesperson and his manager to initiate a dialogue regarding the skills this person requires. This discussion may be subjective but it would still serve the purposes well.

RETENTION STRATEGIES

I think retention strategies are nothing more than figuring out why people would leave in the first place, and doing something about it proactively. If a company were already providing a good salary, working environment, benefits, chances for growth and so forth, why would anyone leave whom the company wants to or should retain.

Quite often, I have seen companies lose good people because they were frustrated or because they found better opportunities elsewhere. My philosophy is that if a person were happy working somewhere she would not look around for better opportunities. Hence, anyone looking for better options shows her unhappiness. When that happens, when the person finally decides to leave, the managers scurry back and forth trying to persuade the person to stay. Offering promotions and showing the prudence in reversing the decision. Alas, it does not work every time.

The tricky thing is to be able to retain this person while not disgruntling the rest of the employees, who may view the favors bestowed upon this person as favoritism. One answer to this question is to put this person on a fast track to growth, enabling this person to achieve greater heights in a shorter span of time. However, this presupposes that, one, there is growth, or room for growth and two, this person consistently proves her mettle. Here the question may arise again why the most important of all roles or projects are given to this person. Here organizations may show flexibility in the sense that they take her off this fast track wherever she falls behind, and she may pick up right from that spot once she can show that she is up and running again, so to speak.

Proactively speaking, this practice may be extended to everyone regardless of the subjective opinions any line manager may have in terms of who should or should not be groomed for the top spot. I think the decision to assess a person's capability at the beginning of one's career is unfair at best. Whether a person is deemed a generalist or a specialist should become evident because of performance at various roles and projects. Everyone needs to be able to given a chance to show what he is made of. The practice of putting anyone on the fast track based on performance is a good decision and reeks of merit based assessments.

Supposing that excellent performance is rated as 'A' and anyone who gets that rating for two consecutive years gets on the fast track and continues till her performance, for whatever reason, slides to 'B' for a year. If she regains the 'A' rating, she goes back on the fast track and so forth. This requires objective performance assessments because everything related to a person's career growth would depend on it.

MANAGING TRANSITIONS

In view of all this information, and the shape of things to come, HRP process must be able to address the shifts in policy regarding hiring, training, and performance evaluations etc. It must also be able to redefine the jobs as their focus may shift from a functional to a process orientation. It should address how people's careers and performances will be managed in such an organization.

FROM FUNCTIONAL TO PROCESS ORIENTATION

How will work change as a production manager, who was responsible for meeting the production targets now becomes responsible for getting the products to the distributors? This requires an understanding of the following model, which I would like to call *'The Model for Re-inventing Work.'* It is simple:

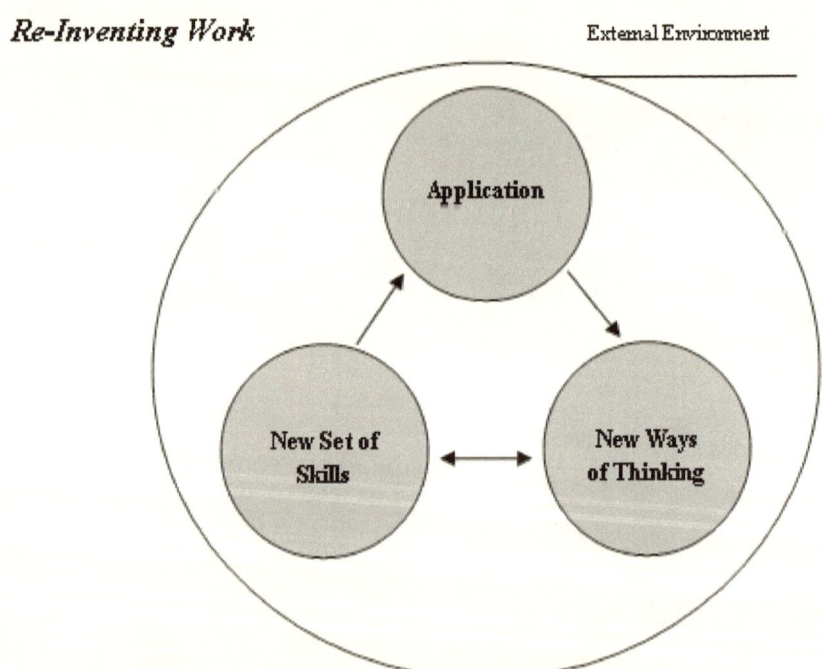

The first step would be to start thinking anew about what it is you are supposed to do and how. Keeping in mind that everyone's job is to make the organization effective, as a supply chain manager, your job is to get the products to the distributors. This involves a team of people from various departments and specializations who would be contributing their expertise. Together all of you would be completely in charge of buying raw materials, overseeing production, controlling costs and quality, managing transportations and so forth. It is a much-enlarged role than any of the individual roles played previously. Hence, it would require a new kind of thinking, which would enable one to grasp the complexities involved. The second step would be to get or acquire the new skills essential for success at this job. Perhaps if previously you were used to working alone and making independent decisions, now you would need to get used to working within close groups and having to make collaborative decisions. It would require a change of mindset and team working skills and interpersonal skills would be tested to the limits. Finally, once your thinking has changed and you have become reasonably adept at newfound skills, you would need to apply them.

HR people need to play a very crucial role in this transformation. They need to redefine the job and assess what skills would be necessary for a person to have in this job in order for her to succeed. They would then have to redesign the performance and reward management system accordingly. They would need to redefine the career management framework within this new setup. They would also need to pay a visit to their compensation and remuneration policies and adjust them according to the career growth patterns that will emerge.

The involvement of every employee would be crucial for the success of this transition. It would have to start by the top man's clarification regarding the future of the organization, and the effects of the proposed changes on everyone. Then there would need to be a selection of the people who would be playing the new roles in the new setup. And, answer the question about what would happen to those who are left out because of this selection process. However, whether or not people are made redundant because of this change would largely depend upon the company's philosophy, vision, and way of working. Hence, if a company believes that no one should be made redundant, it could come up with many other creative solutions to employing extra people rather than just letting them go.

MANAGING GROWTH IN HORIZONTAL ORGANIZATIONS

It is a misunderstanding that the hierarchical way is the only way of managing people's growth. A company, which transforms itself to being process oriented, could still manage people's career growth. In a hierarchy, the growth looks like this:

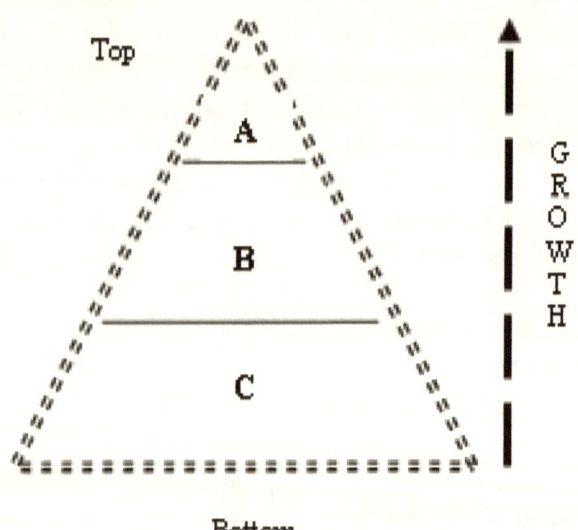

In a horizontal organization, the growth would also be lateral. However, it could still be seen as growth if people can jump from grade to grade after completion of successful tenures or tours of duties. For instance, in the example above, a person sees his progression as he moves from grade C to

Journey Man's Diary-Volume I

grade B. Hence, he is promoted to being a regional manager from being an area manager. In a horizontal organization, he can go from being supply chain manager to being the relationship manager while staying in the same grade. Only after he has successfully completed certain numbers of projects over time, and has attained a healthy overall performance rating, would he be promoted to the next rung of the ladder. This Career Ladder could graphically look something like the following:

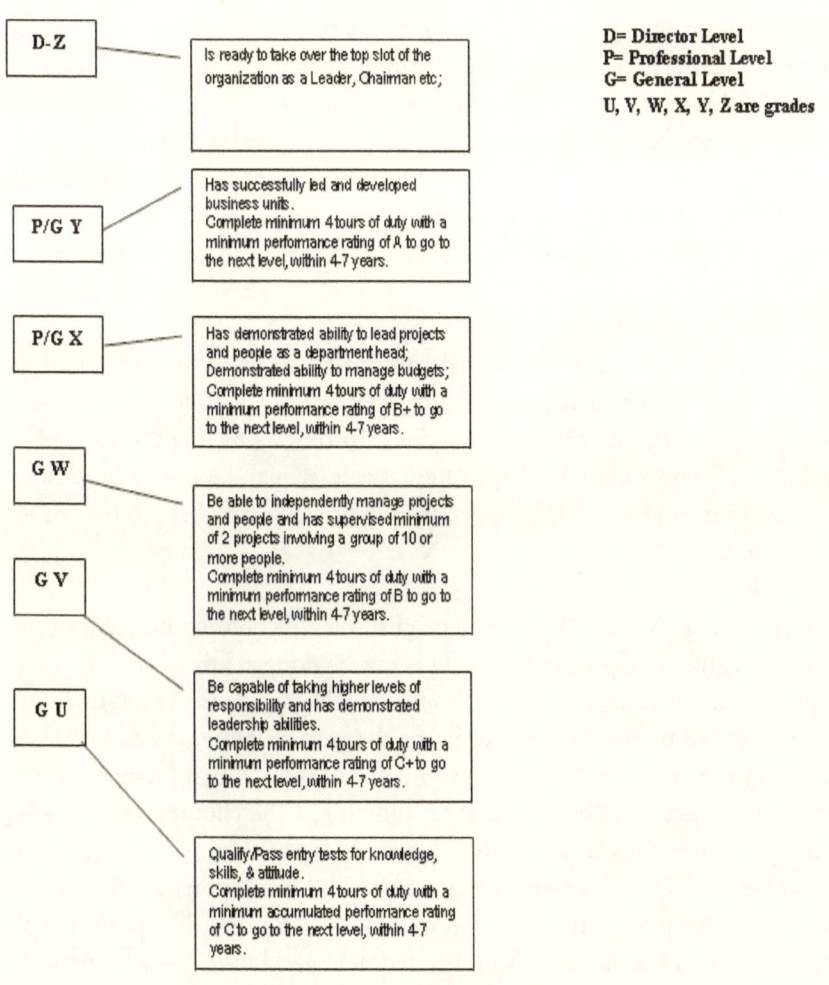

As can be seen from the diagram, no mention of a function has been made. Hence it applies equally well to either specialists or generalists as far as their growth in the organization is concerned in any given department, function or process. Keeping in view that this is generic formula; organizations can adapt and add on to it according to their realities and aspirations.

For instance, from a generalist point of view, a person can come in at G-U say in the marketing department or in the corporate brand & image management group. He has to, then, complete a minimum of four tours of duty or projects within his assigned role or job. While his performance will be evaluated in terms of his job description, his promotion would depend upon the success rate of the projects assigned to him. He can move up the ladder if he is very competent within four years, though he can take up to seven to prove his worth.

If he cannot perform as per the desired level, he may be transferred to another department such as finance or relationship management group, if he meets their criteria. There he may find a project, which raises his level of performance and moves him up. Alternatively, it may be mutually decided between him and his line manager(s) to help him find another job in another organization.

As he moves up, he takes on more generalist roles of coordinating, budgeting, communicating as a project leader. This can be done at any of the functions or processes. However, once he gets to the P/G X grade level, he has to decide to go in either the professional cadre or the general cadre. If he chooses to become a P-X, it means he becomes a functional head say in finance and the rest of his growth will be in that same function. If he chooses to be a G-X, it means he has chosen to remain a generalist and is eyeing the top slot of becoming a CEO. In both cases, the training and development activities will vary for both options in terms of grooming. In the case of a professional, more input that is functional would be required and in the case of generalist, more leadership input would be required.

Similarly, for a specialist, she may enter at the G-U level but unlike her generalist counterpart, move cross functionally. Hence, if one is hired as an internal management development specialist, she may move across all borders, working on various improvement projects and delivering results just like anyone else. However, her growth would largely be in the professional cadre and while over 25 years of career she may hold the same title of *'management development trainer'* or *'training facilitator'*, she would still be able to enjoy the benefits of a P-X, Y, or Z.

CLOSING REMARKS

Hence, the HRP process is not just evaluating the market supply and organizational demands. It is much more than that. It is about balancing organizational growth and needs with people's growth and needs. It is about forecasting the changing environment and pre-empting the changes. It is about taking proactive steps to encounter these changes and at the same time, keeping the organization's productivity alive.

THIS THING CALLED CULTURE

It is tragic that usually the top team of any company or organization gets to define or publicly comment upon this thing called organization culture. In my view, the people working in the drenches should be asked what they think the culture of their organization is like. I think that would be more accurate. I believe their view is of more importance than the high-sounding statements issued from the board. Since these people are far removed from the action and the consequences of their decisions, it is ironic that they are regarded as the experts on their organization's culture. They do not know; they cannot know what the real culture is because they belong to an elite class. The people below who are affected by the decisions and actions taken at the top define the real culture.

I would not like to get into defining what culture is. A much more qualified number of researchers and academics are in a better position to do so. All I will assert here is that how people behave, think, and act within any organization, group or community is all a part of this thing called culture. People behave, think, and act in certain ways because of their interpretations of what goes on around them, what decisions are taken which affect them, and how, in a company's context, their line managers treat them, or their perception of it. If there is any truth to the assertion that behavior begets behavior, then culture is nothing more than acting out of certain beliefs people may have or have developed within an organization. Hence, if an organization is simply a bunch of people getting together to achieve something, then culture is the collective 'psychodrama' played out.

We talk about changing the culture and many different ways are used to do so. I believe that it is simply a matter of changing the mindset and attitudes of people. However, it is not as simple as that. Changing people's attitudes, perceptions, beliefs etc., requires them to open up and communicate openly. I think it is also the essence of becoming a learning organization. If people cannot communicate openly and honestly, if they do not possess the will to stand up to the truth, etc, the organization can never truly become a learning organization.

BALANCING GROWTH

Within the context of culture, and changing a culture, must come the question of balancing growth. The reason we talk about 'wanting to change' a culture is to improve the organizational performance so that it can grow. Growth has its own issues relating to people. For instance, if a company is growing fast people can expect to move up quite quickly, but when it is not, people may still want to move up quite quickly. Hence, balancing people requirements with organizational requirements must be a leader's and a change agent's prime focus.

Organizing, developing and changing than becomes synonymous with growth and effectiveness, because all the changing, organizing, and developing that we do is to grow and become more effective. All of this needs to be aligned with the organization's direction and future. In this context, the hopes and aspirations of individuals working within this organization must be viewed as important as the goals and targets the organization sets up for itself.

Finally, and again within an organization's context, the HR department must play a pivotal role in enabling the organization to achieve its goals. Hence, in my view, HR should show the most flexibility so that the organization can become what it wants to be.

One of the most fundamental causes of the situation described above lies in the structure of this organization. It has grown in time to become a hierarchy and everything else has just grown around it as moss on trees. What would happen if we changed the structure? What would happen if we did away with the pyramid?

Let us say that instead of the pyramid we have a ball with various cores. This is what it would look like:

The Organizational Ball

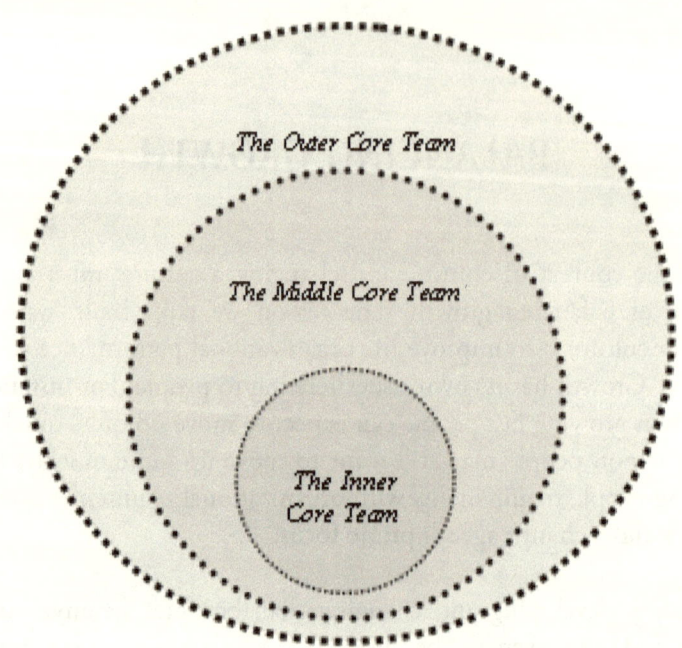

The outer core team would consist of factory workers, administrative staff, supervisors, and team leaders. The middle core would consist of junior, middle, and senior managers. Finally, the inner core would comprise of directors and CEO. This would reduce the hierarchy to three levels. In terms of grades, there would only be Grade **O** (for Outer Core), Grade **M** (for middle core), and Grade **I** (for inner core). This could also become the skeleton of the organization, around which everything else grows.

From growth perspective, the people in this organization would have only three levels to jump. Each level could have almost the same entitlements with a few differences, which would be there only as 'incentive' to work harder/smarter. In this scenario the outer core team (OCT for short) would have one objective. The middle core team (MCT for short) would have one objective, and the inner core team (ICT for short) would have one objective. All, of course, linked to the over all organizational objectives, which are linked to the organizational vision.

In this scenario, the functional fiefdoms would come to naught. Each person is a team member and some are playing the additional roles of team leaders in any number of given projects. The performance management system would also be tailored to measure the team performance as well as individual performance on a project-to-project basis over the financial year. Based on which the people would get their yearly salary increments. However, criteria for moving from one level of responsibility to another would have to be different.

KNOWLEDGE MANAGEMENT

What an idea to have an organization without the traditional understanding of what is known as 'Structure'. Applying our formula of re-inventing work, let us rethink our notion about organization structure.

There are some businesses, such as most of the production-based organizations, whose work is of a continuous or repetitive nature. Then there are other types of companies, as consulting firms, whose work is largely project based. There are also a number of instances when a line manufacturer needs to initiate a new product, which is treated as a project, and instances where within a project based company work is of repetitive nature, like the accounting department of say a consulting company. If we were to apply the concepts of knowledge management to any type of organization, would it be the same? Would it be effective in both scenarios? To answer that we have to first understand what KM is all about.

To create a culture where knowledge management can thrive requires a non-traditional structure, because the principles of KM cannot thrive in an organization which is hierarchy bound. Considering that we have a lose/tight organization where there are three core teams and no 'titles' or 'designations' which signify the importance of any one person in rank over another. In addition, the work is done on a project basis, the first HR related issue would come in terms of benefits and compensations. One way to resolve this issue is as follows:

Team Level	Responsibility Level	Compensation	Benefits
Outer Core Team	Tactical, Operational	1-10 units	All
Middle Core Team	Tactical, Leadership	12-22 units	All
Inner Core Team	Strategic, Leadership	24-34 units	All

The fact that anyone possessing a special kind of knowledge can move from one project to another based on that knowledge applies within each team. Anyone who performs well within say the outer core consistently and lives up to the standards of leadership requirements at the middle core level can be moved up after fulfilling pre-requisite training and development. Alternatively, anyone in the outer core who possesses intimate knowledge of a subject can be moved in the middle or even the inner core team on a project, and enjoy the increment as a bonus until such time the project is completed. At that time, that person can move back to his/her normal role/position. Knowledge Management cannot survive as a management tool in a hierarchy bound bureaucracy where roles and positions are fixed with specific job responsibilities, grades etc.

Another feature that makes pyramid a structure is called 'Reporting Relationship.' The man on the top has people reporting to him who in turn have other people reporting to them and so forth. KM needs a place where no such lines exist. Yes, you would require leaders, but not a CEO, or VPs or Directors etc. What you would have is a team in the inner core working out the strategic issues such as dealing with the media, financial institutions etc, but not a specific role of a CEO as such. This would be a consensus-based model.

[1] Rev. Martin Luther King Jr. (1929-1968), Baptist minister and civil rights leader, won the Nobel Prize in 1964 for his nonviolent struggle for racial equality. The following speech was delivered on August 28, 1963, at the Lincoln Memorial in Washington D.C. to some 200,000 blacks and whites holding a demonstration. Some ten civil rights leaders-after meeting with President John F Kennedy-addressed the crowd. It was generally agreed that the King's Speech was the highlight of the demonstration.

[2] Built To Last by Jim Collins

[3] Corporate Donkeys by Haroon Khalid

[4] Developing Management Skills, 3rd Edition, David A Whetten, Kim S Cameron.

[5] Type Talk at Work by Otto Kroeger, Tilden Press Book

www.ingramcontent.com/pod-product-compliance
Lightning Source LLC
Chambersburg PA
CBHW022023170526

45157CB00003B/1336